Maintaining Generational Freedom

McDougal & Associates
Servants of Christ and Stewards of the Mysteries of God

Maintaining Generational Freedom

Student's Manual

Crystal Callais and Lorraine Foret

Maintaining Generational Freedom
Copyright © 2020, 2021— Crystal Callais and Lorraine Foret
ALL RIGHTS RESERVED

Unless otherwise noted, all Scripture quotations are from the *Holy Bible, King James Version,* public domain. References marked "AMP" are from the *Holy Bible, Amplified Version* copyright © 1954, 1958, 1962, 1964, 1965, 1987 by The Lockman Foundation, La Habra, California. References marked NIV are from *The Holy Bible, New International Version*, copyright © 1973, 1978, 1984, 2011 by Biblica, Colorado Springs, Colorado.

Published by:

MCDOUGAL & ASSOCIATES
18896 GREENWELL SPRINGS RD
GREENWELL SPRINGS, LA 70739
WWW.THEPUBLISHEDWORD.COM

McDougal & Associates is dedicated to spreading the Gospel
of the Lord Jesus Christ to as many people as possible
in the shortest time possible.

ISBN 978-1-950398-26-3

Printed in the U.S., the U.K. and Australia
For Worldwide Distribution

These lessons were inspired by the Holy Spirit.

Our freedom was bought at the cross by the blood
of the new covenant (Matthew 26:28).

Our hope is that through this study
you will receive the tools to help you
reach the freedom and breakthroughs
you have prayed for
and the ability to MAINTAIN THEM!
— *Crystal and Lorraine*

Acknowledgments

Most of all, we want to give thanks to our Lord Jesus Christ for discipleship, for opening our eyes to revelations in the Scriptures through the Holy Spirit, and for leading us to come to an understanding of the reasons for the trials we were experiencing, whether through personal dreams, visions, prophecies, etc. Also, for revealing to us what and who we are truly fighting and just how to war a good warfare. We want to thank Him for the peace and comfort we experienced through His placing certain people in our lives at the times we needed them the most, as our true hearts were being exposed to us. Mostly, we want to acknowledge our Heavenly Father for opening our hearts to catch a glimpse of understanding the depths of His great love for people everywhere and the measures He will go to to see them reconcile their hearts back to Him. Through all the personal struggles we endured, the tears, and the resistance from others, You showed us both just how the enemy of this world operates. You showed us that we have a choice and what true freedom can feel like. We will always be sincerely grateful that You leave the ninety-nine to go after the one.

We thank our readers from the bottom of our hearts. We are grateful for the opportunity, the ability, and the strength to write what we have endured, as well as received in our own life in a way that encourages others in their relationship with the Father. This journey the Lord God has taken us on in this process has forever changed our lives and our family lineage!

We would also like to acknowledge those who helped us with encouragement and with the editing and formatting of this curriculum. We must especially thank:

- *Kim and Vanessa Voisin, our pastors and dear friends*: Thank you for seeing what God was doing in our lives and for nurturing that within us and for the countless hours spent in coaching us in your office along the way. Thank you both for being obedient to the Father and encouraging and helping us walk through the opportunities God has opened in our lives. We are grateful to the Lord for placing our families with you both as our pastors. When we wanted to give up, no matter what it took, neither of you would let go of us. For the last twenty years you have both spoken and imparted things into our lives and our children's lives. We are forever grateful for having such amazing, true shepherds of the Father in our life.

Lorraine would also like to personally thank:
- *Kurt Foret, my husband, and my family and closest friends*: Thank you all for the tremendous support and patience as I went through the hardest season of my life. You encouraged me not to stop, and I am truly grateful.

- *Earl Hutcherson, my father*: Thank you, first, for provoking me to read and study the Word of God for myself. You challenged me to find the truth of what the Scriptures truly meant and unknowingly taught me to dig deep within the Word of God.
- *Wilma, my mother:* Thank you for teaching me through your lifestyle. I learned that God is still real and alive through watching you question Him through the loses of two sons. Through all the whys, the hows we experience in life, you never lost your faith in the Father. Through life's events, you unknowingly challenged me to search the Word for my own answers.
- *Denise Triche, a missionary and dear friend*: You showed me what it looks like to be still and sit at the feet of Jesus and listen, and you truly inspired me to understand the fullness of the Trinity.
- *Crystal, my daughter:* Thank you for all the countless hours of going back and forth while composing this curriculum together with mutual respect and understanding as a team.

Crystal would also like to personally thank:
- *Russell Callais, my husband and forever friend:* Thank you for encouraging me to keep going and to share my heart with others, and for the time you spent to help me gather my thoughts. Thank you for believing in me! Thank you for being willing to share parts of your life as well through this curriculum. I love you!
- *Kurt and Lorraine Foret, my parents:* Thank you for believing in me and for agreeing to put our personal lives and revelations out for the world to see. You have instilled in me that with God all things are possible. You have helped me to dream and not limit myself. Thank you for encouraging me along the way!
- *My siblings and my children:* Thank you for believing in me and helping me dream. Thank you for encouraging me to keep going!
- *The countless friends and mentors who speak into my life:* Thank you. You have encouraged me to be real when I'm talking and writing. I'm grateful for your friendship and belief in me, to keep reaching and to allow God to work and shine in and through my life.

Endorsement

I have personally been blessed, and our congregation as well, by Lorraine Foret and Crystal Callais' ministry leadership. Through this amazing revelation God has given them, they uncover and identify the traps people fall into that keep them from fulfilling their God-intended destiny. Countless Christians are snared and even paralyzed by things they don't even realize are inside their heart. This unique teaching, I believe, will propel you into unprecedented levels in God. It is a must read and a most important investment any individual can make. This book will challenge you to break through old paradigms and will inspire every area of your walk with God.

Rev. Kim F. Voisin, PH,D
Pastor, Vision Christian Center
Bourg, Louisiana

Contents

	Introduction	11
	The Fruit of the Program	13
	Requirements	16
	CHART: The Connection Between the Trinity and Man	18
	CHART: The Garden of Eden	19
1.	The Importance of Applying the Whole Study	21
2.	Am I a Captive or a Prisoner?	31
3.	Am I a Successful Warrior in God's Army?[1]	41
	CHART: Psalm 23	47
4.	Introduction to the "Steal" Door[2]	51
5.	Adam and Eve and the Garden of Eden	59
	Jehovah-Jireh	67
6.	Satan and Eve	73
	Jehovah-Shalom	81
7.	Adam	87
8.	Introduction to the "Kill" Door[3]	103
	CHART: Hebrews 12 (Our Warnings)	106
	Jehovah-Rophi	108

---
1. From this point on, daily journaling of the Word is required.
2. This covers your emotions, impulses, spoken curses, vows, etc.
3. This covers sickness, spiritual idolatry, reality and hornets.

9. Cain and Abel 113
    CHART: Four Biblical References on Anger and Offense 124
    Jehovah-Tsidkenu 125

10. Spiritual Idolatry 131
    CHART: The Tree of Life 136
    CHART: The Tree of the Knowledge of Good and Evil 137
    CHART: The Tree of Spiritual Idolatry 143

11. Introduction to the "Destroy" Door[4] 145
    Jehovah-Shammah 150

12. Four Judgments in Ezekiel 153

13. Noah and Three Generations 163
    Jehovah-M'Kaddesh 169

14. Malachi 1 and 2 173

15. Malachi 3 and 4 185
    Jehovah-Nissi 192

16. Our Atmosphere 197

    Afterword 206
    Other Books by Crystal Callais and Lorraine Foret 207
    Author Contact Page 211

---

4. This covers heart circumcision, reconciliation of offenses, sonship, and finding our true identity in Christ.

INTRODUCTION

This study was inspired through revelations by the LORD God through the Holy Spirit. We were seeking the LORD for insight into how and why we, along with other Christians, suffer to get breakthroughs and keep them. It's easy to get defeated and feel as if there is no point in pushing through. We were studying the Scriptures and searching for the Promised Land within ourselves and our family. We wanted breakthrough in certain areas, and we struggled finding it.

We often hear teachings about generational blessings and generational curses. The Holy Spirit started to reveal to us (me and my mom, separately at the beginning) motives and thoughts we had with mindsets and actions behind them that led to history repeating itself in our lives. He began to show us how to reverse the patterns and mindsets to receive the freedom we desired.

The LORD started to show us the legal rights Satan had (that we or generations before us had handed to him) to attack us and follow our children. The Holy Spirit opened our eyes to how things pass from one generation to the next. Through prayer and application, we have seen miracles before our eyes within our own family, and this has completely changed the dynamics of how we live, interpret, and function in life. This has also been true for those with whom the LORD God allowed us to share these truths. Throughout the lessons we will share testimonies as examples of what and how things pass down from one generation to the next, how to stop the patterns and how to enjoy life the way the Bible says we should.

Jesus Christ died on the cross for us to experience Heaven on Earth now, but we have to access it and then maintain it. The Scriptures say that we are to walk out our salvation through fear and trembling (see Philippians 2:12). This study will bring you to an understanding of the mindsets in which you operate. We will discuss the three doors Satan uses and how we can close those doors and lock them, keeping him out! We hope these lessons and their application inspire you and give you the tools you need to get the breakthroughs you have always dreamed of for your own life.

Each lesson has corresponding homework and applications. These studies are only meant to be a basic foundation for you to grow from. You will need to take this information into prayer and ask the Holy Spirit how to apply it to your own life and situation. As you do, you will go from head knowledge of the Scriptures and promises of God to heart knowledge, but this will happen ONLY if you apply yourself to the prompting of the Holy Spirit as He leads, guides, and opens your ears, eyes, mind, and especially, your heart.

The Spirit of the LORD GOD is upon me;
because the LORD hath anointed me to preach good tidings unto the meek;
he hath sent me to bind up the brokenhearted,
to proclaim liberty to the captives,
and the opening of the prison to them that are bound.
Isaiah 61:1

We are anointed to do the work of the Lord through the Holy Spirit. Jesus spent most of His time teaching and healing in the synagogues. We are called to bind up the brokenhearted, proclaim liberty to the captives, and open the prison door for those who are bound. These people are sitting in our churches; they are sitting in the same room with you.

- Nothing in this study will say that you are not saved. This is not about salvation.
- These are things that, even being saved, we can deal with.
- We are in a battle that is not against flesh and blood.

WE WANT TO REVEAL A PLAN TO YOU,
A PLAN THAT YOU MAY NOT KNOW IS EVEN HAPPENING,
A PLAN THAT YOU ARE THE TARGET OF,
A PLAN THAT AFFECTS YOU,
A PLAN MEANT TO HURT AND DESTROY YOU.
SOMETIMES THE PLAN WILL SUCCEED,
AND SOMETIMES THE PLAN WILL FAIL.

IN YOUR BATTLE,
IS THE ENEMY WINNING?
OR
ARE YOU WINNING?

The Fruit of the Program

Here are some typical comments we have gotten over the past few years from people who have applied the tools they learned through this study. For you, this is a list of possibilities. All of these blessings and more are available for you too!

"I moved from being lukewarm and complacent with God to wanting more."
"I now read and journal from the Word, and before I didn't have that desire."
"My faith has grown."
"I now have a deeper understanding of how and why Satan attacks me."
"My trust in God has gotten deeper."
"I now have a deeper understanding of the Word and its application to my walk with God."
"I now hear God's words and voice MORE CLEARLY."
"I learned how to get back to the garden."
"My discernment has gotten stronger."
"I have started to see in the Spirit realm."
"I understand submission now (to God and to other people)."
"I went from religion (works) to relationship and grew in my ability to recognize demons."
"I now have deeper convictions."
"I am now walking in my calling more and am stronger than before."
"I discovered my calling for the first time."
"My prayer life has become active and more powerful."
"I experienced Jehovah-Jireh through being laid off due to the coronavirus."
"I have seen my marriage improve."
"I am experiencing more peace."
"My thought pattern has changed."
"I can see life more clearly."
"I have had a restoration of relationships."
"I realized the power of my words."
"I was healed of allergies."
"I learned to separate people from actions."
"I experienced more Heaven on Earth than I had before."
"I now react through counsel and self-control instead of impulse."
"I learned to be a peacemaker instead of a peacekeeper (which is a people-pleaser)."
"I watched my kids' reality change."
"I'm no longer a prisoner within myself."

"I now have the ability to expose and not to suppress."
"The study has changed the dynamics of our family lineage."
"I learned communication."
"I became bolder when God speaks to and through me."
"My dreams have become more vivid and detailed."
"I am now able to use my authority in the Spirit realm."
"The spirit is more real to me now than the physical."
"I have developed stronger leadership qualities."
"I came to realize that the battle isn't always mine."
"I have seen and experienced power behind breaking generational curses."
"We realized that Masonry was part of my husband's grandfather's life and seen sickness, jealousy, and other things fall off of us when it was renounced."
"I feel joy again."
"I learned true forgiveness."
"I became more compassionate toward others."
"Sickness and disease are coming to an end in my life."
"This study removed my insecurities and lies I believed from my early motherhood."
"I learned humility."
"I learned to prioritize."
"I now feel loved."
"I have more patience."
"My child's life is now more structured and settled."
"I have seen God bring finances and prosperity."
"I have started to believe in areas that I couldn't before."
"I am seeing answers to prayer manifest faster."
"I grew content."
"I now stress less."
"I can now accept blessings."
"I was set free from pornography and lust."
"I am free from guilt."
"I was freed from a gambling habit."
"I am free from the need to control everything."
"I have been set free from low self-esteem and low self-worth."
"I am free from anger."
"I am free from unforgiveness."
"I am free from rejection."
"I am free from migraine headaches."
"I am free from insecurities and limiting myself in how God uses me."
"I was freed from the fear of betrayal."

"I am now free from people's expectations."
"I was freed from a spirit of bitterness."
"I am free from criticism."
"I was set free from rebellion against an authority figure."
"I was delivered from distrust."
"I am free to a new degree from co-dependency."
"I am free from anxiety."
"I am free from pride."
"I have been freed from jealousy and envy."
"I am free from fear."
"As a father, I received a revelation of how important my walk with God is to my children, in order for them to experience freedom."
"I am now seeing Jesus in control."
"I now see where the enemy was able to steal, kill and destroy in my life."
"I now see how my behavior and habits caused unhappiness and discontentment to others."
"Now I realize why my parents (and others) do what they do."
"I now want to stay in the river and not on the banks."
"I now see the truth of how God and the enemy work."
"I have had a physical healing manifest in my body, a healing of my hips and knees."

Through the guidance of the Holy Spirit, this study can change your life too!

TO MAINTAIN THE FREEDOM WE AIM FOR:

- I will hold up the standard of holiness explained on the next page. This will provide a standard for my life to be able to maintain my freedom after the study is finished.
- I agree to let go of what I had yesterday and be open to all the Lord God has for me today.
- I commit to the Lord to journal from the Word daily and apply all that I read. (This is the renewal process for your mind. Our mind is something we are to daily wash and renew).
- I will be part of the Body of Jesus Christ and work as a group with this class.
- I will tithe, as found in Malachi 3, to (my home church).
- I will NOT allow myself to be offended for any reason, at any time, or with anyone.
- I will NOT leave the study because of an offense and cause others to stray.

This study will bring up other areas in your life God wants you to deal with, and you will have a choice to make.

REQUIREMENTS:

- I will NOT allow myself to be offended for any reason, at any time, or with anyone.
- I will NOT leave the study because of an offense and cause others to stray.
- I will do all assignments within the time given. (This makes me a doer of the Word.)
- I will attend all meetings, unless preapproved by _____ (who is the leader of the study) with a good reason given, or I am out. (This study and class will become a priority for a lifestyle change needed to maintain freedom).
- I understand that this is not a Bible Study FOR KNOWLEDGE and that attendance and participation ARE NOT optional. This is the foundation of a LIFESTYLE CHANGE.
- I must maintain an open mind.
- I understand that no children are allowed in the study!
- I agree to follow the Blog and comment when needed (if the leader of the group chooses to make a blog).

Notice: This study will draw a lot of your time and focus. I advise not to be heavily involved in other studies while participating in this study.

_____   _____
PARTICIPANT   LEADER

Date: _____   _____

Our leadership standard of holiness is found in 2 Kings 3:9-19. These are ditches that need to be dug first.

Leaders MUST:
1. Have a private and public prayer life.
2. Be given to the study of the Word of God.
3. Be a giver to God's work (in tithes and offerings).
4. Respect the pastor and his wife in speech and action.
5. Have a positive spirit of faith (no murmuring and complaining).

Leaders MUST NOT:
1. Be argumentative.
2. Listen to worldly music.
3. Be given to tobacco or any type of drugs or alcohol.
4. Be given to movies with cursing or nudity.
5. Be offensive to others in speech or action.

The Connection between the Trinity and Our Promised Land and Our FULL Redemption

The God Head =	**God, the Father**	**Jesus, the Son**	**The Holy Spirit**
Our three-part connection to the God Head	Our Soul (mind, will, emotions)	Our Body (Jesus was made flesh)	Our Spirit (bears witness)
_____ The way Satan attacks us	_____ He steals by getting us to believe and speak contrary to the Word of God.	_____ He kills us because we do have physical bodies to take care of in this world.	_____ He destroys us because of what we do, tolerate, or ignore affects more than just us!
What the three doors look like that Satan uses to attack us	_____ Our soul (emotions) dictates our feelings, feelings dictate our speech, speech opens the door by _____ _____	_____ Our physical health is compromised when we open the door with _____ _____	_____ These are the things that are spiritually broken then _____ _____ to continue to pass through.
How to close the doors	Mentally – _____ Physically – _____ Spiritually – _____	Mentally – _____ Physically – _____ Spiritually – _____	Mentally – _____ Physically – _____ Spiritually – _____
How to lock the door when we close it	_____ We keep it locked by _____ _____ Romans 12:2 – _____ Romans 1:25 – _____	_____ We keep it locked by _____ By being healed _____ Deut. 7:20 – _____ Heb.10:35-39 – _____	_____ This is locked by what we _____ operating and not _____ it to pass in our lifestyle. Men – _____ power
What redemption (closed doors) would look like	- Full fellowship with God, our Father - No guilt and no shame - I hear God, and God hears me.	Going from religion to a relationship Going from head knowledge to heart knowledge	- Direct communication (complete surrender, being Spirit-led) - Complete power in the Spirit realm (getting off the throne of my heart)

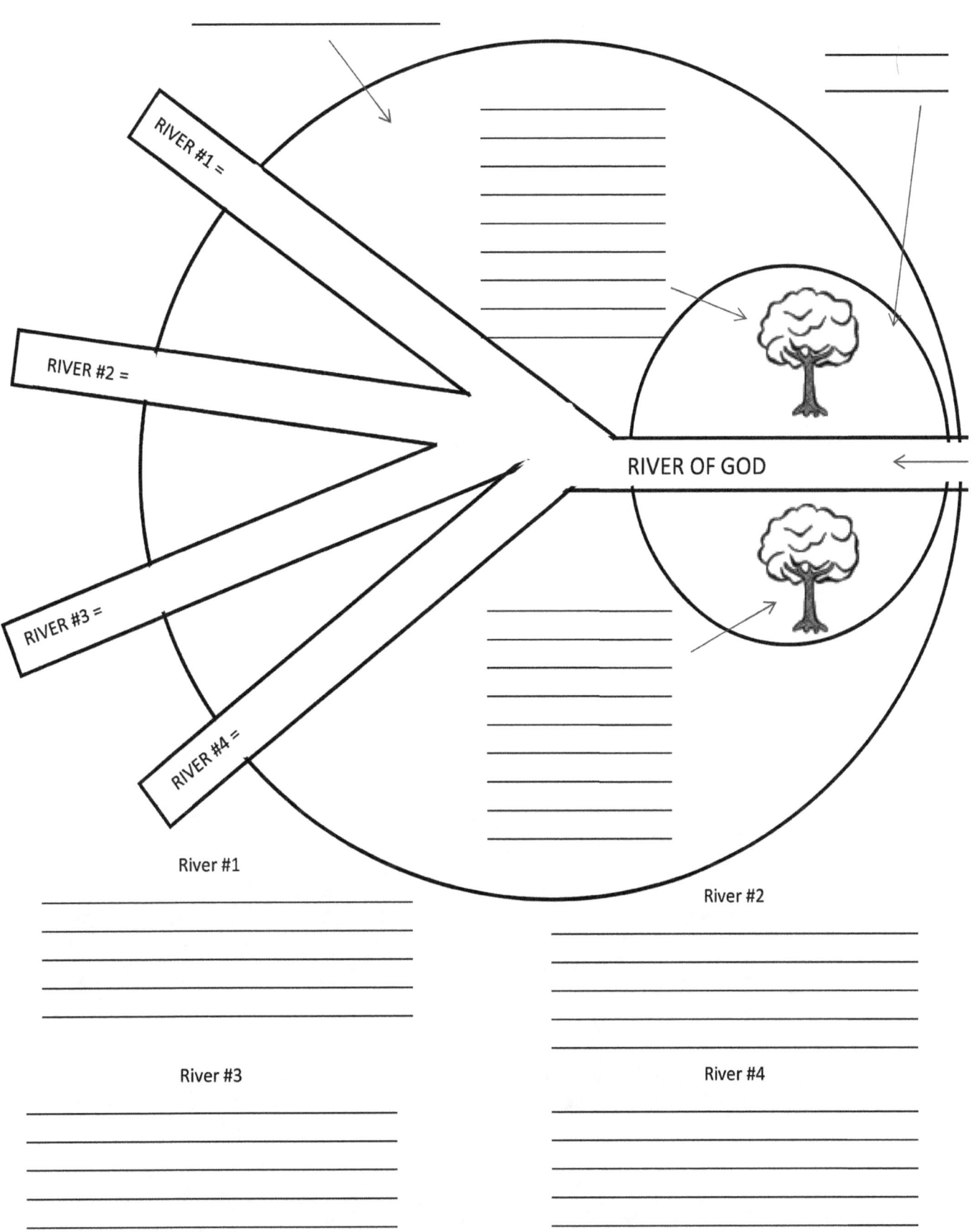

— Notes —

Chapter 1

The Importance of Applying the Whole Study

Romans 7

<u>The apostle Paul used a picture of marriage and adultery in the physical to show us what spiritual idolatry looks like.</u>

Matthew 12:43-45
- The unclean spirit left. IF his house was kept clean and empty, seven more wicked spirits would come.
- Jesus said, *"The last state ... is worse than the first."* (These words are in red, indicating the words of Jesus.)

John 5:1-14
- The man by the pool was healed.
- Jesus later found him in the temple and said to him, *"Sin no more, lest a worst thing come unto thee."*
- You have to change from your current actions.

_____
_____
_____
_____
_____
_____
_____

Hebrews 10:26

"For if we sin willfully after that we have received the knowledge of the truth, there remaineth no more sacrifice for sins."

_____
_____
_____

1 Corinthians 10:21

"Ye cannot drink of the cup of the Lord, and the cup of devils: ye cannot be partakers of the Lord's table, and of the table of devils."

- You can't do good things today or for two days and then go back to your old way of living and expect nothing to change.
- You will now be accountable to start the process of purging out your old life and not live according to the flesh anymore.

_____
_____
_____
_____
_____
_____
_____
_____

Genesis 4:6-7
- Do what's right, and you will be accepted.
- Don't, and sin lies at your door.

_____
_____
_____
_____

Ephesians 4:26-27

"Be ye angry, and sin not: let not the sun go down upon your wrath: neither give place to the devil."

- Emotion isn't a sin; it's what you do with the emotion that could lead to sin.
- The colon after wrath means that if you do act wrongly based on your emotions and fall into sin, the consequences of it will be giving a foothold to the devil.

_____
_____
_____
_____
_____
_____

Homework
- Complete the definition page to the best of your ability.
- Return a signed agreement (page 16).
- Bring money to cover the purchase of the book (unless otherwise purchased).
- Follow the Blog (if the leader of the study chooses to create one).

DEFINITIONS

Define these words using *Webster's* or a good online dictionary. Do your best to find Bible references in which the word or the meaning of the word is used. Then define the words from a biblical point of view (referring to a good Bible dictionary).

INIQUITY
Webster's: "*gross injustice or wickedness, violation of right or duty; wicked act or sin*"

Bible References: Exodus 20:5 "*I ... am a jealous God, visiting the iniquity of the fathers upon the children to the third and fourth generation of them that hate me.*"
This is part of the Ten Commandments.

Biblical Meaning: "*to crook, literal or figuratively; to bow down, pervert*"
Other words used: *perversity, depravity, iniquity, guilt, or punishment*

OFFENSE
Webster's: "*a violation or breaking of a social or moral rule. A transgression of the law. The cause of a transgression or wrong. The feeling of resentful displeasure.*"

Bible References: Matthew 18:7 "*Woe unto the world because of offences! for it must needs be that offences come; but woe to that man by whom the offence cometh!*"

Biblical Meaning: "*stumbling block, obstacle, snare, a trap-stick (movable trigger)*"
Root meaning: "*bend a knee (figuratively in worship)*"

PRISONER
Webster's: _____
_____
_____

Bible References: Isaiah 61:1_____
_____
_____

Biblical Meaning: _____
_____
_____

CAPTIVE
Webster's: _____
_____
_____

Bible References: Isaiah 61:1_____
_____
_____

Biblical Meaning: _____
_____
_____

IDOLS
Webster's: _____
_____
_____

Bible References: _____
_____
_____

Biblical Meaning: _____
_____
_____

LEGALISM (FROM A ROOT WORD MEANING LAW)
Webster's: _____

Bible References: _____

Biblical Meaning: _____

STRONGHOLD
Webster's: _____

Bible References: <u>2 Corinthians 10:3-4</u>_____

Biblical Meaning: _____

INTRUSION
Webster's: _____

Bible References: <u>Jude 4 *"certain men crept in UNAWARES." Unaware,* in other translations, is *"enter secretly," "to go unnoticed."*</u>

Biblical Meaning: _____

PERMISSION
Webster's: _____
_____
_____

Bible References: _____
_____
_____

Biblical Meaning: _____
_____
_____

LEGAL RIGHTS
Webster's: *legal + rights—* _____
_____
_____

Bible References: Colossians 2:13-15 Biblically, it's the handwriting of ordinances the enemy has against us.
_____

Biblical Meaning: _____
_____
_____

COVENANT
Webster's: _____
_____
_____

Bible References: _____
_____
_____

Biblical Meaning: _____
_____
_____

UNFORGIVENESS
Webster's: _____

_____

_____

Bible References: _____

_____

_____

Biblical Meaning: _____

_____

_____

DEBT
Webster's: _____

_____

_____

Bible References: _____

_____

_____

Biblical Meaning: _____

_____

_____

WILDERNESS
Webster's: _____

_____

_____

Bible References: _____

_____

_____

Biblical Meaning: _____

_____

_____

TRADITION

Webster's: _____

_____

_____

Bible References: Mark 7:9-13 _____

_____

_____

Biblical Meaning: _____

_____

_____

TRESPASS

Webster's: _____

_____

_____

Bible References: _____

_____

_____

Biblical Meaning: _____

_____

_____

PERVERSE

Webster's: _____

_____

_____

Bible References: _____

_____

_____

Biblical Meaning: _____

_____

_____

— Notes —

Chapter 2

Am I A Captive Or A Prisoner?

Luke 19:10 and Matthew 18:11 say the same thing. Write them out on the lines below:

_____
_____
_____
_____
_____

Isaiah 61:1-4

"The Spirit of the Lord God is upon me;
because the LORD hath anointed me to preach good tidings unto the meek;
he hath sent me to bind up the <u>brokenhearted</u>,
to proclaim liberty to the <u>captives</u>,
and the opening of the prison to them that are bound [<u>prisoners</u>]." Verse 1

<u>Biblically meek (poor),</u> meaning "poor in spirit"
<u>Biblically a captive,</u> meaning "to take captive, carry, lead away"
<u>Biblically a prisoner,</u> meaning "to tie, bind, imprison, to yoke or to hitch, to obligate"

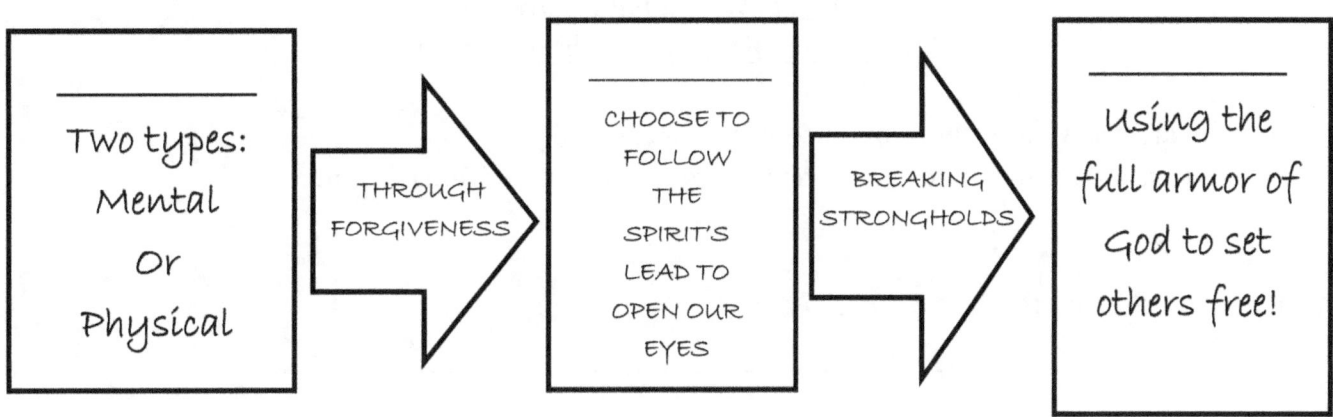

You can transfer from any box in any order; this is just the order we strive for!

Being a prisoner and a captive are both stages in which we are wounded Christians.

The _____ of the Promised Land or the _____ or _____ of a warrior can cause you to fall back into prisoner.

- Captives and prisoners, from the outside, look the same.
- When you're a captive, you can pray or speak for things to break or change, and they will!
- When you're a prisoner, you need repentance and forgiveness to release you or bring you back to the captive state.

CAPTIVE

Isaiah 5:13-25
Why we become captives:

(Vs.13) _____

_____

(Vs.21) _____

_____

(Vs.24) _____

_____

(Vs.25) _____

_____

2 Peter 2:19

"... while they promise them liberty, they themselves are the servants of corruption: <u>for of whom a man is overcome, of the same is he brought in bondage</u>."

- You are a slave to whatever controls or masters you.
- You are a slave to whatever you revolve your time or decisions around.

What are you a slave to?

_____

_____

2 Peter 2:20-22
- After they escaped, they returned and were entangled.
- Knowing truth, they turned from God's commandment.
- They were like a dog returning to its vomit.

Where have you known or experienced freedom to later have the opportunity to return to the same bondage you were once delivered from, perhaps even in a different form?

_____
_____
_____

Isaiah 42:6-8
- The Lord sets us free and OPENS our eyes!
- ONLY the Lord can show us and others (you cannot try to force information on someone who isn't ready to hear it).
- You can't get out of prison with closed eyes.
- You can open your eyes by giving the Lord the glory instead of idols (vs.8).

Do you ask the Holy Spirit to show you where your eyes are closed or where you are ignorant?
Are you willing to allow the Holy Spirit to show you where you keep or give the glory or honor to another?

_____
_____

Deuteronomy 7:20

*"Moreover the Lord thy God will send the hornet among them,
until they that are left and hide themselves ... be destroyed."*

How does the Lord your God show you what's hidden from you?

_____
_____
_____
_____

**** The intrusion God allows Satan to send us may be to show us what's blocking us from truly inheriting the Promised Land! ****

PRISONER

We will discuss two types of prisons we get into:

_____
_____

Prison #1: God Puts Us into a PHYSICAL PRISON

Matthew 18:21-35
  Master—God; *servant* or slave—me
- The Master (God) locked <u>them</u> in the prison because of unforgiveness (see vs.25).
- *Them* refers to their family—wife and kids—because of his actions.
- Forgiveness is the key to the prison cell!
- It's a choice and MUST come from the heart (see vs. 35).
- You have to choose not to get offended or to carry an offense!

Did you put yourself in prison for unforgiveness?

_____
_____
_____
_____

Did you inherit a prison cell?

_____
_____
_____
_____

What does prison look like?

_____
_____
_____
_____

Prison #2—We Place Ourselves in MENTAL PRISONS

2 Corinthians 10:3-4
> *"For though we walk in the flesh, we do not war after the flesh:*
> *(For the weapons of our warfare are not carnal, but mighty*
> *through God to the pulling down of strong holds)."*

Stronghold—"to fortify, through the idea of holding safely; a castle (figuratively, argument), fortress, anything on which one relies." Some translate this word as "prison."

Romans 1:18-25
What is the process of being darkened and a stronghold developing?

_____
_____
_____
_____
_____
_____

Deuteronomy 7
- This whole chapter is on deliverance and freedom.
- Vs. 5 shows us how to destroy a demonic stronghold.
    ° An altar is "a place for sacrifice" (symbolic of our wounds).
    ° Altar idols are just idols (symbolic of a Band-Aid for our wounds).
    ° Groves are areas of trees dedicated to idolatry (symbolic of the lies that keep us protecting).
    ° Images are also idols (symbolic of the justifications people see and what we base our decisions on).

(space for drawing)

James 1:22

> *"But be ye doers of the word, and not hearers only,*
> <u>**DECEIVING**</u> *your own selves."*

- By not being a doer of the Word, we build our own walls at times.

**Healing happens when we are hungry enough
to seek it out and brave enough to confront our fears!**

Homework
- Complete the definitions that follow.
- Start keeping a list of the breakthroughs and revelations you receive in your quiet time with the Father.
- Continue building several houses, strongholds, as the Spirit leads you.

DEFINITIONS

Define these words using *Webster's* or a good online dictionary. Do your best to find Bible references in which the word or the meaning of the word is used. Then define the words from a biblical point of view (referring to a good Bible dictionary).

FORGIVENESS
Webster's: _____
_____
_____

Bible References: _____
_____
_____

Biblical Meaning: _____
_____
_____

COMMANDMENTS
Webster's: _____
_____
_____

Bible References: _____
_____
_____

Biblical Meaning: _____
_____
_____

CURSE
Webster's: _____
_____
_____

Bible References: _____
_____
_____

Biblical Meaning: _____
_____
_____

SPIRIT
Webster's: _____
_____
_____

Bible References: _____
_____
_____

Biblical Meaning: _____
_____
_____

SOUL
Webster's: _____
_____
_____

Bible References: _____
_____
_____

Biblical Meaning: _____
_____
_____

Look up Exodus 34:7, Psalm 32:5, or other scriptures that deal with iniquity, transgression, and sin. After you define each, tell me the difference between them.

INIQUITY
Webster's: _____
_____
_____

Biblical Meaning: _____
_____
_____

TRANSGRESSION
Webster's: _____
_____
_____

Biblical Meaning: _____
_____
_____

SIN
Webster's: _____
_____
_____

Biblical Meaning: _____
_____
_____

In your own words, what is the difference between these three words?
_____
_____
_____
_____
_____

— Notes —

Chapter 3

Am I A Successful Warrior in God's Army?

Ephesians 6:1-9
- Talks about submission.
- Talks about being the same at all times.
- Talks about our actions.

_____
_____
_____
_____
_____
_____
_____
_____

Ephesians 6:10-12
Against whom do the Scriptures say you are fighting?

_____
_____
_____
_____
_____
_____
_____
_____
_____
_____
_____
_____

Maintaining Generational Freedom | 42

Ephesians 6:13-20
How are we to fight the enemy?
_____
_____
_____

List the parts of the armor this passage of scripture reveals IN ORDER with your own explanation:

The First Piece of Armor: _____
- Truth is the Word of God.
- The first tool given to us!

_____
_____
_____
_____

Worn correctly IF: _____
_____
_____

Worn incorrectly IF: _____
_____
_____

The Second Piece of Armor: _____
- In the physical, the Roman guards would tie the bottom of the breastplate to the belt to hold it in place during battle.
- The breastplate covers our hearts.
- We shrink our breastplate when we allow offenses to be resurrected.

_____
_____
_____
_____

Worn correctly IF: _____
_____
_____

Worn incorrectly IF: _____
_____
_____

The Third Piece of Armor: _____
- Our feet walk on the ground. Our feet walk in the way of OUR FOUNDATION.

_____
_____
_____
_____

Worn correctly IF: _____
_____
_____

Worn incorrectly IF: _____
_____
_____

The Fourth Piece of Armor: _____
- Your mindset or what and how you believe.
- In the battle line, it was a soldier's responsibility to care for his own shield, just as it is your responsibility today.
- Shields could be joined together to make a wall of protection or put over your head as a cover.
- This is the only weapon we use WITH other soldiers.

_____
_____
_____
_____

Worn correctly IF: _____
_____
_____

Worn incorrectly IF: _____
_____
_____

Maintaining Generational Freedom | 44

The Fifth Piece of Armor: _____
- We are saved by the blood of Jesus, BUT do we keep everything under the blood of Jesus?
- Our head wears the helmet. Our mind (our thoughts) is the area of battle with the enemy.
- We are told to bring every thought captive to the obedience of Christ (see 2 Corinthians 10:5).

_____
_____
_____
_____

Worn correctly IF: _____
_____
_____

Worn incorrectly IF: _____
_____
_____

NOTICE:

_____ feed your _____ which feed your _____.
   (transgression)   (iniquity)   (sin)

The Sixth Piece of Armor: _____
- It is the Word of God (written and spoken).
- The sword is in our speech.
- THIS IS THE ONLY OFFENSIVE WEAPON WE HAVE; THE REST ARE DEFENSIVE.

_____
_____
_____
_____

Worn correctly IF: _____
_____
_____

Worn incorrectly IF: _____
_____
_____

What will stop you from becoming an effective warrior for God?

_____
_____

THIS IS HOW GOD PICKS HIS ARMY (Deuteronomy 20:5-9).

List the things that stop you from reaching the warrior stage.

Vs. 5: "And the officers shall speak unto the people, saying, What man is there that hath built a new house, and hath not dedicated it? let him go and return to his house, lest he die in the battle, and another man dedicate it."
_____
_____

Vs. 6: "And what man is he that hath planted a vineyard, and hath not yet eaten of it? let him also go and return unto his house, lest he die in the battle, and another man eat of it."
_____
_____

Vs. 7: "And what man is there that hath betrothed a wife, and hath not taken her? let him go and return unto his house, lest he die in the battle, and another man take her."
_____
_____

Vs. 8: "And the officers shall speak further unto the people, and they shall say, What man is there that is fearful and fainthearted? let him go and return unto his house, lest his brethren's heart faint as well as his heart.
_____
_____

Vs. 9: "And it shall be, when the officers have made an end of speaking unto the people that they shall make captains of the armies to lead the people."

Leviticus 18:24-28

_____
_____

_____
_____

It doesn't matter what position you are in! You're not just fighting for yourself. You are fighting for your whole lineage! You are empowered by the Holy Spirit to set your whole family lineage **FREE**!

What stage are you in? (circle one)   Prisoner   Captive   Warrior

Now that you know your position, make a list of things you need to do to progress to the next stage, ultimately ending in Warrior!

For example:

If you are a prisoner:
    Forgive _____ for _____ (this releases you).
    Forgive yourself for _____ (this takes you out of work mode).
    Forgive God for _____ (this reconciles you back to God).

If you are a captive:
    List the things you see running in your family.
    Ask the Holy Spirit to show you how to let go and get free from them.

If you are a warrior:
    Who are you helping to pull from prisoner or captive?
    Are you using the full armor of God?
    Which part of the armor are you using or not using?

To be a successful warrior, we have to know the Lord our God intimately for who He is, NOT who we think He is!

This is also why journaling is an important habit. Journaling keeps your mind washed and reconciled back to our Heavenly Father!

LET'S START THE PROCESS OF PURGING
OUR HEART OF IDOLS!

Psalm 23:1-6

(1)	THE LORD IS MY SHEPHARD I SHALL NOT WANT.	**Jehovah-Rohi**, my Shepherd = to the voice of a stranger I will not harken! **Jehovah-Jireh**, my Provider = meets my needs.
(2)	HE MAKETH ME TO LIE DOWN IN GREEN PASTURES: HE LEADETH ME BESIDE THE STILL WATERS.	**Jehovah-Shalom**, my Peace = I need to learn to rest in the LORD.
(3)	HE RESTORETH MY SOUL: HE LEADETH ME IN THE PATHS OF RIGHTEOUSNESS FOR HIS NAME'S SAKE.	**Jehovah-Rophi**, my Restorer and Healer = He heals my soul. **Jehovah-Tsidkenu**, my Righteousness = For His name sake, not mine.
(4)	YEA, THOUGH I WALK THROUGH THE VALLEY OF THE SHADOW OF DEATH, I WILL FEAR NO EVIL: FOR THOU ART WITH ME; THY ROD AND THY STAFF THEY COMFORT ME.	**Jehovah-Shammah**, Thou art with me, omnipresent = in the valley, everywhere I go, at my home and work. The LORD is in my sphere of influence!
(5)	THOU PREPAREST A TABLE BEFORE ME IN THE PRESENCE OF MINE ENEMIES: THOU ANNOINTEST MY HEAD WITH OIL; MY CUP RUNNETH OVER.	**Jehovah-Nissi**, my Banner = my victory over every enemy. **Jehovah-M'kaddesh**, my Sanctification = part of setting me apart for the priesthood; with oil He is anointing me.
(6)	SURELY GOODNESS AND MERCY SHALL FOLLOW ME ALL THE DAYS OF MY LIFE: AND I WILL DWELL IN THE HOUSE OF THE LORD FOREVER.	

Homework
- Complete the definition pages that follow.
- Continue keeping a list of the breakthroughs and revelations you receive in your quiet time with the Father.
- Check the Blog and comment when asked (if one was created).

DEFINITIONS

Define these words using *Webster's* or a good online dictionary. Do your best to find Bible references in which the word or the meaning of the word is used. Then define the words from a biblical point of view (referring to a good Bible dictionary).

HUMILITY
Webster's: _____
_____
_____

Bible References: _____
_____
_____

Biblical Meaning: _____
_____
_____

RIGHTEOUSNESS
Webster's: _____
_____
_____

Bible References: _____
_____
_____

Biblical Meaning: _____
_____
_____

WORSHIP
Webster's: _____
_____
_____

Bible References: _____
_____
_____

Biblical Meaning: _____
_____
_____

HONOR
Webster's: _____
_____
_____

Bible References: _____
_____
_____

Biblical Meaning: _____
_____
_____

RESPECT
Webster's: _____
_____
_____

Bible References: _____
_____
_____

Biblical Meaning: _____
_____
_____

— Notes —

SUBMIT

Webster's: _____
_____
_____

Bible References: _____
_____
_____

Biblical Meaning: _____
_____
_____

FOLLOWER

Webster's: _____
_____
_____

Bible References: _____
_____
_____

Biblical Meaning: _____
_____
_____

Chapter 4

Introduction to the "Steal" Door

1 Peter 5:8

"Be sober, be vigilant; because your adversary the devil, as a roaring lion, walketh about, seeking whom he may devour."

What are some characteristics of a lion?

_____
_____
_____
_____
_____
_____
_____
_____
_____
_____
_____
_____
_____
_____
_____

Just as a physical lion, Satan waits for you to be separated from fellow believers for whatever reason, and that makes you vulnerable to his attacks. He uses the same tactics over and over because we seem to fall for them every time.

Satan's attack includes: Stealing through OUR _____ _____
    (Thief)   Killing through _____ _____
                    Destroying through _____ _____

Iniquity

More than simply an act of sin; it is the character of the action.

It is a system of behavior, a way of life, one that seems to have a life of its own.

In Exodus, when iniquity is mentioned in the commandments, it means "a crook (literal or figuratively), to bow down."

The Hebrew word translated "iniquity" is also translated as "perversity," "depravity," "iniquity," "guilt" or "punishment."

Proverbs 26:1-2

"The curse causeless shall not come." (vs. 2)

Four types of curses we will discuss as we go through this first door:

#1: _____ brings a curse.
(Deuteronomy 28 and Jeremiah 11)

#2: _____ brings curses.
(1 Samuel 15:22-23, Proverbs 17:11 and 1 Corinthians 11:27-30)

#3: _____ _____ are brought on us by what we allow others to say over us and also by what we THINK about ourselves.
(Philippians 4:8, Romans 8:5 and Isaiah 54:17)

#4: _____ _____ is our mindset. Whatever we believe about ourselves, we will become.
(Proverbs 23:1-7)

"Jesus Christ the same yesterday, and to day, and for ever."
Hebrews 13:8

INNER VOWS

Matthew 5:33-37
- A warning not to make vows
- Read Judges 11 and see Jephthah's vow.

_____
_____
_____
_____
_____
_____

Are you living with the result of broken vows or impulsive vows you've made? Have you been unable to discover why you seem to be circling the same mountain again and again? Could it be that you are being faced with vows you or your forefathers made and don't realize it? Ask the Holy Spirit to show you where you have made inner vows or promises to yourself or others. If you seek and ask the Holy Spirit, He will show you. Don't dismiss the names and thoughts He drops into your spirit.

_____
_____
_____
_____
_____
_____

JUDGMENTS

Matthew 7:1-6

"For with what judgment ye judge, ye shall be judged:
and with what measure ye mete, it shall be measured to you again." Vs. 2

- Whatever decision you make and whatever you use to make that decision will come back to you.
- You reap what you sow.
- Whatever judgment you put on someone else you will live by.

_____
_____
_____
_____

SOUL TIES

Luke 14:26-27 (Words of Jesus)

"If any man come to me, and hate not his father,
and mother, and wife, and children, and brethren,
and sisters, yea, and his own life also, he cannot be my disciple.
And whoever doth not bear his cross, and come after me,
cannot be my disciple."

Maintaining Generational Freedom | 54

If our soul holds our emotions, why would Jesus tell us to hate our family?

_____
_____
_____

What would your family have to do with you following Jesus or not following Jesus?

_____
_____
_____
_____

Ephesians 4:20-28
According to Ephesians, when we get saved, what are we told to do?

_____
_____
_____
_____
_____
_____

Why should we watch how we react and pay attention to our emotions, being careful not to feed the flesh, for this can lead us to sin? Rather, we must seek to follow the leading of the Spirit.

_____
_____
_____
_____
_____
_____
_____

Revelation 2:18-29 (words of Jesus)

Verse 20 says, *"... because thou sufferest that woman Jezebel."* *Sufferest* means "to let be, permit or leave alone." He is telling the church, "You tolerated her."

Verse 21: She had time to repent and did not.

Verse 22: *"Cast her into a bed ... EXCEPT they repent of their deeds."*

Verse 23 talks about her children. God is telling us that He searches our heart and mind. He repays *"according to your works."*

Verse 24 says, *"... as many as have not this doctrine [instruction], and which have not known the depths [mystery, deepness] of Satan."*

Verse 25, *"But that which ye have already, hold fast till I come."* *Hold fast* means "to use strength, seize, or retain (literally or figuratively)."

But what do the Scriptures say we get if we overcome and keep God's works unto the end?

Vs. 26 _____

Vs. 27 _____

Vs. 28 _____

Proverbs 13:2-3

"A man shall eat good by the fruit of his mouth:
but the soul of the transgressor shall eat violence.
He that keepeth his mouth keepeth his life:
but he that openeth wide his lips shall have destruction."

- You will eat the fruit of your lips.
- Every time you talk, imagine seeds being planted that you or your descendants will one day reap the fruit of.

Homework
- Continue keeping a list of your breakthroughs and revelations as you receive them in your quiet time with the Father.
- Check the Blog and comment when asked (if one was created).
- From here onward, daily journaling and quiet devotional time with God is required.
- Complete the definition page that follows.

DEFINITIONS

Define these words using *Webster's* or a good online dictionary. Do your best to find Bible references in which the word or the meaning of the word is used. Then define the words from a biblical point of view (referring to a good Bible dictionary).

THORN
Webster's: _____
_____
_____

Bible References: _____
_____
_____

Biblical Meaning: _____
_____
_____

THISTLE
Webster's: _____
_____
_____

Bible References: _____
_____
_____

Biblical Meaning: _____
_____
_____

PRIDE
Webster's: _____
_____
_____

Bible References: _____

_____

_____

Biblical Meaning: _____

_____

_____

WITCHCRAFT

Webster's: _____

_____

_____

Bible References: _____

_____

_____

Biblical Meaning: _____

_____

_____

DISCIPLE

Webster's: _____

_____

_____

Bible References: <u>John 8:31</u>_____

_____

_____

Biblical Meaning: _____

_____

_____

SERVANT
Webster's: _____
_____
_____

Bible References: <u>John 8:34</u>_____
_____
_____

Biblical Meaning: _____
_____
_____

Chapter 5

Adam, Eve and the Garden of Eden

To truly understand how Satan works and what he took from us, we have to go back to where it all started.

We will start in Genesis 1, the Creation, where everything started, and see if we can understand:
- What we were created for.
- What was created for us.
- How the enemy, through deception and disobedience, stole it from Adam and Eve then and still continues to steal it from us TODAY.

WHAT WE WERE CREATED FOR

Genesis 1:26-28
According to Genesis, what was man's responsibility after the Lord God created them?

_____
_____
_____
_____
_____
_____

These four things represent what our total redemption back to Christ looks like. This is what we were created for.

WHAT WAS CREATED FOR US?

Genesis 2-3 then goes on to describe what was created for us:

2:8—The Lord God planted a garden Eastward IN Eden.
2:9—The Lord God made two trees to grow in the midst of the garden.
2:10—This river went through the garden (starting on the east side of the garden) and then broke into four heads:

Maintaining Generational Freedom | 60

2:11—The first river was Pison, meaning "increase."
- This river had gold, onyx and stone, bdellium in it.
- (river of _____)

2:13—The second river was Gihon, meaning "bursting forth."
- (river of _____ _____ ___ ___, peace or God's goodness, cup overflows)

2:14—The third river was Hiddekel or Tigris, meaning "rapid."
- (river of _____ _____ _____)

The fourth river was Euphrates, meaning "fruitfulness, breaking forth."
- (river of _____ _____ _____, _____ _____)

AN INTERESTING FACT:
The first two rivers have disappeared off the map, but you can still find the Tigris and Euphrates rivers on maps today!

Man's responsibility (the lifestyle we were created to live) from Genesis 1:28 correlates with the rivers we were designed to have flow THROUGH us.

The responsibilities mentioned in Genesis 1:28 were to:
- Be fruitful (river # _____)
- Multiply (river # _____)
- Replenish the earth, which is to reproduce oneself (river # _____)
- Subdue the earth and have dominion over all (river # _____)

There are ways to either open the river up or to close it off from flowing and operating in our lives.

The First River—Increase
- Our responsibility, given in Genesis, is to multiply.
- *Multiply* means "to increase in whatever respect, whether it is money, time, talent, friends, etc."

Malachi 3:8-12
    Open—_____
    Closed—_____

Adam, Eve and the Garden of Eden | 61

Matthew 6:19-24
   Vs. 19—If you store up on Earth, thieves _____ ____ and steal it. This is a closed river.
   Vs. 20—If you store up in Heaven, thieves ____ _____ _____ ____. This is an open river.
   Vs. 22—Your eye is the light (lamp) to your body.
   Vs. 23—If your eye is light, you are light. If your eye is evil, you are full of darkness.
   Vs. 24—You cannot serve two masters. You cannot serve both God and mammon (money).

   If your _____ is on money, you struggle releasing money to God because it has a _____ on you, referring to ownership. If your _____ is on God, you don't struggle releasing money to Him because you _____ what He will do with it.

      ***The key to unblocking this river, allowing it to flow through our lives, is _____.
      In return, my responsibility in this river is to _____!**

The Second River—Bursting Forth, which means you can't hold it in. Your cup overflows.
- Our responsibility, given in Genesis, is to replenish the Earth.
- *Replenish* means "to fill or be full of."

We are all full of something. We can be full of God or full of ourselves.
   Open—_____
      Psalms 23
   Closed—_____
      Malachi 1:14a

      ***The key to unblocking this river, allowing it to flow through our lives,
      is who I _____, _____, and am _____ to.
      In return, my responsibility in this river is to _____ _____.**

The Third River—Rapid
- Our responsibility, given in Genesis, is to subdue and have dominion, which we do through the Holy Spirit's guidance, through prayer and speech, trusting in God and not in man.
- *Subdue* means "to bring into bondage, positively to conquer."
- *Dominion* means "to tread down, prevail against."
- We are to control and govern our reality instead of our reality controlling us! We do this with prayer and trust in God and not in man.

Prayer – Philippians 4:6
　　Open—_____
　　Closed—_____

Trust – Matthew 16:15-19
　　Open—_____
　　Closed— _____

　　*** The key to unblocking this river, allowing it to flow through our lives, is _____ and _____. In return, my responsibility in this river is _____ my atmosphere through prayer and authority.

The Fourth River—Fruitfulness, which means "breaking forth."
- Our responsibility, given in Genesis, is to be fruitful.
- *Fruitful* (in Genesis) means "to bear fruit, branch off."

Proverbs 11:24-26
　　Open – _____
　　Closed – _____

Jeremiah 17:7-10
- Trusting in the Lord keeps good fruit flowing.

Matthew 25:14-30
- Give the testimony of ALL the life you were dealt and watch the river open up wide!

　　***The key to unblocking this river, allowing it to flow through our lives, is _____ _____ _____ by reproducing ourselves in others, being transparent, NOT in our own strength (pride or false humility), but through the Lord God's strength (humility). In return, my responsibility in this river is to be _____ _____ _____ _____, which is the fruit of the Spirit, not wild grapes, which is a fruit of the flesh.

Genesis 2:15-18

These verses come after the LORD God described the four rivers. This is where the LORD God took man and put him in the garden to dress and keep it!

What could the tree of knowledge represent to us today?

_____
_____
_____
_____

After man partook of the tree, he was sent out of the garden, and the LORD God tells us why! Genesis 3:22-23 says, *"And now, lest he put forth his hand, and TAKE ALSO [STEAL] of the tree of life, and eat, and live for ever: therefore the LORD God SENT HIM FORTH from the garden of Eden, to till the ground from whence he was taken."*

So, man was sent out to prevent him from *"taking also"* or stealing from the Tree of Life. We were created to get wisdom from the LORD God. Adam and Eve decided to get wisdom on their own and take it rather than trusting in the LORD God to give it to them.

Romans 5:12-21

Because of Adam and Eve, we inherited a death, both physically and eternally speaking.

Verse 14 mentions *"Adam's transgression."*
- *Transgression* here means "a violation, to go contrary, violate a command."
- Could Adam's transgression have been abandoning his trust in the LORD God and believing the lie (mental transfer, when his loyalty changed).
- He went from trusting in the LORD God to trusting in his own ability of getting wisdom. He could have talked with the LORD God, but, instead, he took (or stole) and ate, breaking his covenant with the LORD God of eternal life.

Verse 15 says, *"Through the offence of one many be dead."*
- *Offence* means "a deviation from the truth."
- Because Adam deviated from the truth of who the LORD God was to him, it brought death.

Verse 19

> *"For as by one man's disobedience many were made sinners,*
> *so by the obedience of one shall many be made righteous."*

- *"One man's disobedience"* refers to Adam.
- *"The obedience of one"* refers to Christ.

If we were to reword verse 19 the way we speak today, it might sound like this:
> *"One man's disobedience [self-trust, independence, or co-dependence]*
> *brought sin [generational curses]. The obedience of One [Spirit-led or*
> *interdependent with the LORD] shall make many righteous [generational blessings]."*

Verse 20

> *"Moreover the law entered [came in secretly],*
> *that the offence [deviation of the truth] might abound [to exist in abundance].*
> *But where sin abounded, grace did much more abound."*

- *"Came in secretly"* sounds like an intrusion.
- The offense is within us (in our hearts) toward the LORD God, which will cause us to partake of the tree of knowledge.

But whatever is in us, WILL manifest in the physical because we create our reality by what we say and what we hold as truth in our hearts.

HOW THE ENEMY STEALS FROM US

Genesis 3:1-19

3:1—Satan used _____ on Eve.
- ALL SATAN CAN DO TO US!

3:3—The woman _____ to God's instruction when she said, *"Neither shall ye touch it."*
- The woman first twisted God's words.

3:4-5—Satan took the truth and _____ to it: *"Ye shall be as gods [judge/ruler], knowing good and evil."*
- Satan twisted God words, offering woman a chance to be soul-led and trust in her own discernment and wisdom rather than God's.

3:6—The woman decided (with her physical eyes) that it was *"good for food"* (*"pleasant to the eyes"*) and trusted in her own judgment.

Adam, Eve and the Garden of Eden | 65

3:7—Their eyes were opened, and shame came upon them.
   Because of shame, they covered themselves _____ _____ (fig leaves).
   The first thing that hits you when you take of the tree of knowledge is _____.
      Physical and spiritual shame and condemnation!

3:8—They heard the LORD God approaching and hid themselves because of the _____.
- They acted on what they felt (acting out of shame and condemnation).

3:11—*"Hast thou eaten of the tree?"* The LORD God asked man what happened, giving him a chance to confess and repent.
- This was Adam's _____ _____. He was head of the home, woman's covering.

3:12—The man blamed the woman and the LORD God **in the same breath**.
- The second thing that hits you when you take of the tree of knowledge is _____ _____, not my fault.

3:13—The LORD God asked the woman, *"What is this that thou hast done?"*
- This was woman's _____ _____.
- The woman blamed the serpent.

3:14—*"AND THE LORD GOD SAID UNTO THE SERPENT, BECAUSE THOU HAST DONE THIS, THOU ART CURSED ... ."*

How did the LORD God pronounce their consequences given to them for their disobedience?
_____
_____

Satan (vs. 14)

Because thou hast done this, ⟶	• You are cursed according to your deeds (Jeremiah).
Thou art cursed above all cattle, and above every beast of the field; Upon thy belly shalt thou go, and dust shalt thou eat all the days of thy life.	• He was cursed as the lowest of animals, a snake, below every other animal. • He was to move lower than the other animals. • He was brought into condemnation. • Condemned was how he felt.

Everything is created to bear fruit after its kind.

Romans 8:1

> "There is therefore now no condemnation to them which are in Christ Jesus, who walk NOT after the flesh, but after the Spirit."

If we follow our soul, or flesh, we _____ ourselves, leading to isolation. If we follow the spirit, we have _____, which leads to freedom.

Homework
- Continue keeping a list of the breakthroughs and revelations as you receive them in your quiet time with the Father.
- Check the Blog and comment (if one was created).
- Continue journaling daily from His Word.
- Complete the study on God's name Jehovah-Jireh, The Lord is my Provider.

Jehovah-Jireh

Psalm 23:1b *"I shall not want."*
The Lord is my Provider (Genesis 22:14).

What promise has the Lord given me?_____
What am I trusting the Lord for? _____
Where is my faith being tested? (below are a few ideas, circle if they apply)
- Blessings coming? Family getting saved? Promotion? Ministry? My calling or prophecies spoken over me? An opportunity I am believing for? A new job?

Others I can think of:_____
_____
_____
_____
_____
_____
_____

**Write them all down!

Genesis 22:14 is part of the story of Abraham sacrificing Isaac.
The chapter begins, *"And it came to pass AFTER THESE THINGS THAT GOD DID TEMPT ABRAHAM"* (Genesis 22:1, Emphasis added).
- What *"these things"*?
- What caused God to test Abraham?

A Quick Outline of Abraham's Life
(Read the following sections in your Bible as you go through the outline to learn what THESE THINGS were that he got tested on.)

Genesis 12:1—Abram was called to leave his father's house.
- Get out of your country.
- Get away from your kindred.
- Go away from your father's house.
- Go to a land I will show you.

This could be symbolic of us leaving the influences around us and changing our focus to God Himself.

Am I willing to obey God and do what He asks of me? If not, what is stopping me?

_____
_____
_____
_____

Genesis 12:2-3—God's Promise to Abram
- I will make you a great nation.
- I will bless you.
- I will make your name great.
- You will be a blessing.
- I will bless them that bless you.
- I will curse them that curse you.
- In you, all the families of the earth will be blessed.

This could be symbolic of the revelations, prophecies and promises we get from God and then stand on.

Genesis 12:17-20—Abram's actions affected others around him.
- Because his actions were out of "FEAR," he misled and brought plagues on Pharaoh's house.

This could be symbolic of us not understanding God's character or His promises and prophecies and how they will come to pass, so we ACT without asking God what to do.

Can I be trusted to wait on the leading of the Holy Spirit with the revelations or promises the Lord has given me? Or do I ACT and open my own doors, bringing harm on myself and others around me?

_____
_____
_____
_____
_____
_____
_____

Adam, Eve and the Garden of Eden | 69

Genesis 18:22-33—Abraham reasoned for Lot.

Genesis 20:9-13—Abraham's confession of FEAR of losing his life
    (This was the voice he heeded over God's — fear of loss of life.)
That voice caused Abram to make a plan B with his wife when he first left his father's house to obey God. In Genesis 12:12-13, Abram told Sarai what the plan would be to protect his life. They obeyed God with a backup plan.

What is my Plan B, even as I am being outwardly obedient to God? My backup plan will show me where there is a breach of trust in God.

_____
_____
_____
_____

Genesis 21:23-24—Abraham made a vow to no longer DEAL FALSELY with Abimelech, with God as his witness.

When I make a vow, I am brought under that vow, which is a covenant, to be tested and see if I will do what I say! What vows or commitments have I made with God as my witness?

_____
_____
_____
_____

NOW PUT YOURSELF IN ABRAHAM'S TEST:
Read Genesis 22:1-19
In this chapter, Abraham was on his way to sacrifice Isaac.
    (Losing a life was what he feared, and he ended up in self-protection over it.)

Isaac represented the promise God had given Abraham.
        **He was now being tested to see if he would heed other voices as he had
        in the past (and make a PLAN B) or if the vow he had made
        to Abimelech to not deal falsely anymore would stand!**

As you go through the story, think about the areas you have struggled or are struggling in and where you may heed voices other than God's, creating a PLAN B to protect yourself or others.

Maintaining Generational Freedom | 70

Vs. 5—*"Abraham said unto his young men, ... I and the lad will go yonder and worship, and come again to you."*

Remember, it was a three-day journey to get to the place of sacrifice. He was going up to sacrifice the lad, and yet he spoke as if the lad wasn't going to die. Why? Could he have believed God's promise of being a father to the nations more than he believed what reality was saying? Reality said, "You can't have descendants if you kill your son."

When I speak about my promise and desire and the reality of what it is looking like, do I TRUST more in what I see, hear, or think is possible (my reality)? Or do I speak positively, even if reality doesn't seem to line up?

_____
_____
_____

Vs. 6—Abraham laid wood *"upon"* Isaac's shoulders. Your shoulder is where you carry a burden. Abraham allowed the promise to carry the weight.

Do I feel the weight (the job) of making my promise come to pass (working out of legalism because I don't feel worthy of it)? Or do I allow God to carry the weight and open the doors, while I just sit and wait for Him to move?

_____
_____
_____

Hebrews 12:1 tells us to *"lay aside every weight, and the sin which doth so easily beset us."*

What weights do I need to allow Jesus to carry?

_____
_____

Do I trust in the weight more than in the Lord Himself?

_____
_____

As Abraham was going up the mountain to *"obey"* God, he didn't take a lamb with him. There is no "PLAN B" with obeying God.

Am I obedient to God without a plan B?

_____
_____

Vs. 9 states that Abraham *"bound"* Isaac. Isaac was about twenty-five years old. Did he perhaps resist this binding?

When I am at a place of total surrender, putting it all in God's hands, what resistance can I have?
What emotions, lies, thoughts, or people's opinions of me do I have to take captive (see 2 Corinthians10:5)? These are the lies and insecurities Satan throws at me when the pressure is on.

_____
_____
_____
_____

Vs. 12—After God told Abraham what to do, Abraham started to act, but an angel stopped him and said, *"For now I know that thou FEAREST God, seeing thou hast not withheld thy son, thine only son from me."* (You didn't have a PLAN B.) What is fear? Fear is a reverence!

If God says I want you to "give something away," "trust me," or "focus here," do I obey without thinking? Do I reason to see if it's possible for the promise to come to pass if I do this or that? Do I worry what my spouse, friend, or parent will think if I do that? Am I afraid to be obedient to God because I may offend or ripple the water with someone else?
Who do I fear more and why?
Am I worried about other's opinions of me? My image? Or the image of others (causing me to be a prison guard).
What do I protect?

> ***This could be my Plan B that I have to unconsciously protect in case God doesn't come through for me.***

_____
_____
_____
_____

Vs. 16-18—*"thou hast done this thing, and hast not withheld thy son, thine only son: [obedience at all costs], in blessing I will bless thee ... BECAUSE THOU HAST OBEYED MY VOICE."*

Abraham didn't tell anyone what he was doing, so whose voice did he not heed? Could it have possibly been his own or lies from the enemy? Because Abraham didn't have a plan B and didn't heed the voice of fear, he was blessed and multiplied, and the promise of the covenant was able to start to be a reality.

Who or what do I listen to and why? (Remember, Adam heeded the voice of his wife.) Do I heed the voice of another person or even the voice of my walls or fears (idols)?

_____
_____
_____
_____
_____
_____

Adam worked out of his strength, laying himself UNDER a curse, a judgment (see Jeremiah 17:5), because he first heeded the voice of woman (see Genesis 3:17).

Abraham's blessings:
Despite his failure with Ishmael (the first PLAN B), Abraham turned back and obeyed God's voice with Isaac (see Genesis 22:18).

You may be taking the Lord's name in vain or lightly IF you proclaim He is your Provider, and yet you are not heeding His voice and, instead, heeding reality and making a PLAN B!

Chapter 6

Satan and Eve

Genesis 3:15 (AMP)
"*And I will put enmity (open hostility) between you and the woman, and between your seed (offspring) and her Seed; He shall [fatally] bruise your head, and you shall [only] bruise His heel.*"

And I will put enmity between thee and the woman

(_____)

- He sowed division through reasoning, which led to the deception, so that he would reap division through reasoning.
- Reasoning takes place in your soul.
- Your soul is made up of your mind (thoughts) and emotions.
- Reasoning causes us to make a vow, swear an oath, or make ourselves promises (see Ecclesiastes 5:1-7 and Matthew 5:33-37).
- *Enmity* means "hatred, hostile, to treat as an enemy."
- This is a conflict between Satan and the woman.
- *Woman* means "helpmate."
- The woman displays the emotional, feminine quality from the Lord God, His favor, or advice.

Because woman, THROUGH DECEPTION, heeded Satan's voice, leading her to take of the tree and eat, she gave up the Lord God's peace, comfort, and assurance. She traded the Lord God's wisdom, which was clear direction and clarity, for her own judgment. Therefore, we now reap confusion and double-mindedness when we choose to allow discouragement to crush our hopes and dreams. Instead of trusting in the Lord God's abilities, we have a tendency to start relying and trusting in our own strengths. This is where we can end up losing our hope, leaving us with no other alternative, and this leads us into compromise.

Maintaining Generational Freedom | 74

References:

2 Corinthians 11:1-4—(The Amplified Version is helpful in explaining the story.)
_____
_____
_____

James 1:2-8
_____
_____
_____

Matthew 6:24
_____
_____
_____

Have you noticed that when you make a decision, you can have a tendency to doubt yourself? This could be a way that the consequences of the judgment are operating in your life.

And between thy seed and her seed; • Division between Anti-Christ and Jesus

(_____)

It shall bruise thy head, → The _____ enmity (the first part of the judgment),
and thou shalt bruise his heel. → The _____ enmity (the second part of the judgment, prophecy).

Jesus defeated the enemy!

The First Enmity:
"*It*" means to double-mindedness, confusion, being tossed back and forth.
"*Bruise*" means "to crush, gape upon, break, cover, desire."
"*Thy head*" means "my head, thoughts."

The Second Enmity:
"*Thou*," referring to Satan.
"*His*," referring to Jesus.
Satan can come at my head with thoughts, but his proper place is under our feet through Jesus Christ.

2 Corinthians 10:3-5
Vs. 3—We walk in the flesh but don't war in the flesh.
Vs. 4—The weapons of our warfare:
- Our only weapon is _____ _____ (the Word of God). The rest are defensive, for warfare.
- This verse refers to armor. So, we must have our armor on _____ for the battle!
- The sword is the Word of God, but _____ _____ _____ _____!
- It's our job to put those thoughts under His [Jesus'] heel through our loyalty and devotion, returning it back to God. (Our armor is activated through prayer and becomes effective when we are being Spirit-led.)

Vs. 5 tells us to make every thought obey Christ.
- This is _____ _____. God doesn't bring the thought down; we do!

** Ultimately Satan has power (_____ _____) to stir division through our emotions and our mind, which is our soul, if we take from the tree of knowledge and allow ourselves to be _____ _____.**

WOMAN

God blessed man, so He doesn't _____ man!
Let's notice how the consequences of the judgment and the curse of the ground work.

Genesis 3:16 (AMP)
> "To the woman he said, 'I will greatly multiply your pain in childbirth;
> In pain you will give birth to children; yet your desire and your
> longing will be for your husband, and he will rule
> [with authority] over you and be responsible for you.'"

Unto the woman he said, I will greatly multiply thy sorrow and thy conception
- *Sorrow* means "pain, labor, hardship, sorrow, toil, worrisome."
- Comes from a root word meaning "worship, pain, hurt."
- *Conception*, literally or figuratively
    Physically, meaning pain in childbirth
    Spiritually, through our offenses and idols, our emotions are multiplied and intensified.

As women, we have literal pain in childbirth, but there is also an emotional toll. This is saying that our emotions can be intensified to the point of us wanting to worship them. It is an emotional struggle not to be driven by impulse and emotion. Because woman's soul (seat of emotions and mind) drove her to eat of the tree, her consequence for relying in her own strength and wisdom vexed her soul from _____!

How do we vex our soul?
2 Peter 2:8 says that what we see and hear will vex our soul from day to day.

What are some things you see or hear that can vex your soul?
_____
_____
_____

In sorrow thou shalt bring forth children,
- *Sorrow* means "hurt, pain, toil, offense, create, idol."
- (From the same root word as "to worship")
    Physically, referring to pain in childbirth
    Spiritually, through our offense and idols, we create the next generation.

This is why _____ women hold the key to learned behavior.
This is part of the reproduction process.
We spiritually reproduce the next generation to carry the same _____ we have.

We teach our children WITHOUT EVEN REALIZING IT:
- How to guard against certain things or people.
- How to fear what we fear.
- How to self-protect the way we self-protect.
- How to judge or carry themselves the way we do.
- How to talk just like us.
- How to show appreciation and respect the way we do.
- How to respond to people through body language and tones.

This is usually referred to as the grid, or mindset, we look through and process life through.

Satan and Eve | 77

And thy desire shall be to thy husband, and he shall rule over thee.
- *Desire* means "longing."
- *Shall rule* means "to exercise dominion, reign or power."

Adam and Eve were created with equal dominion and power (see Genesis 1:28), but Eve was to be a helpmate. She **was** to feel protected, loved, and taken care of under her husband. Now, however, she COULD feel controlled, not protected or cherished, but rather, dismissed and overlooked, not even a vital partner!

The authority that Adam was given wasn't control but _____! Man was not intended to control woman, but rather, to exercise his power to _____ her atmosphere and protect her from the enemy.

When we choose to be _____ _____ (male or female), we put ourselves BACK under the consequences of the judgment we were delivered from. By being soul-led, we live with the effects of the judgment still operating in our lives. When we trust more in our emotions than in God's truths, we lay ourselves under the consequences of the judgment.

Reference: **Philippians 4:1-7** (To get out from under the consequence of the judgment and back to walking in freedom)

_____
_____
_____

1 TIMOTHY 2:11-15

11. Let the woman learn in silence with all subjection.
- *Learn* means "to be informed, learn by use and practice, to understand."
- *Silence* means "quietness, one who stays home and minds his own work." (Learn to mind your own business.)
- *Subjection* means "obedience" from a root word meaning "to obey, submit to one's control."

We have to learn, by use and practice, by _____ the Word to our lives. We have to learn to submit to another's control. We have to force our soul to submit to the Word of God through the Holy Spirit and become Spirit-led. No more impulses! No more getting in everyone's business! No more giving unsolicited advice UNLESS it's prompted by the Spirit! No more assumptions or incorrectly reading body language! Instead, we must search out the truth in love. We need to use our sword correctly, and we need to learn true submission. Submission is in our obedience.

Maintaining Generational Freedom | 78

12. But I suffer not a woman to teach, nor to usurp authority over the man, but to be in silence.
- *Suffer* means "to turn, transfer, permit, allow."
- *Teach* means "to teach or instill doctrine into one."
- *Usurp authority* means "to govern or use dominion over."
- *Silence* means "quietness, minds his own work."

Once we learn to control our tongue and allow the Holy Spirit to guide us, we are submitting under the Spirit's authority and the authority of our husband. We, as women, are to _____ ourselves.

Reference:
Titus 2:4-5—How should women reproduce themselves in other women?

_____
_____
_____
_____
_____
_____
_____
_____
_____

13. For Adam was first formed, then Eve. 14. And Adam was not deceived, but the woman being deceived was in the transgression.
- *First* means "first in rank or influence."
- *Formed* means "used of a potter, a form, a mould."
- *Deceived* means "cheated, beguiled, of uncertain derivation."
- *Transgression* means "a disregarding or violating, breaking the consciousness of sin to be intensified and the desire for redemption to be aroused."
- *Transgression* comes from a root word meaning "to overstep or to abandon trust."

Adam wasn't deceived, Eve was. The transgression came from the _____!
The root word for *transgression* gives us an idea of what the iniquity was.
Iniquity, which is the offense, is the root reason behind the transgression that leads to the sin (the action).

Example:
Iniquity, meaning IN THE _____ , which causes an offense, is abandoning her trust. (Now she distrusts, and you need to prove something.)

    2 Corinthians 11:3—She gave up the simplicity of her mind.
        Simplicity is "sincere and pure devotion to God."

Transgression, meaning that she allowed or _____ the deception to reason in her mind. Doubting will lead us to become double-minded. It will lead to a divided loyalty and devotion to the LORD.

Sin, meaning she took fruit from the tree, took wisdom because she _____ _____ _____ that the LORD God was holding out on her.

15. Notwithstanding she shall be saved in childbearing, if they continue in faith and charity and holiness with sobriety.

- *Notwithstanding* means "nevertheless."
- *Saved* means "rescued from danger, destruction, healed."
- *Continue* means "remain, abide, endure."
- *Faith* means "conviction of the truth of anything."
- *Charity* means "affection, good will, love."
- *Holiness* means "consecration, purification of heart and life."
- *Sobriety* means "soundness of mind, self-control."

Eve would be saved, rescued from the danger, and healed, if and when she saw the reality she was leaving for others. Just seeing what was happening would _____ save her. The KJV says, "_____" she continues. As a woman, we have a choice: Ignore it and let it continue, or do something about it. We are rescued and made free IF we continue.

Don't stop!

Summary:
- Adam wasn't deceived; Eve was!
- Adam wasn't cheated out of his dominion; he was disobedient. Eve was cheated through deception from her loyalty and devotion that became misplaced.
- Before eating of the fruit of the tree of knowledge, the woman had **full trust** in Adam (as her covering) and the LORD God (as Adam's covering).
- The woman being deceived is the transgression (according to 1 Timothy). The root of the transgression (the iniquity) comes from overstepping and abandoning trust.
- Verse 15 tells us how a woman is to take her soul out from the consequences and the judgment! She will be healed, or rescued, from danger in childbearing because, in reproducing herself (whether biologically or through mentoring), she teaches and holds a mirror to her face, and it allows her to see what she is passing on to her children.
- **This is the key to learned behavior. You cannot clean out your heart before God unless He first shows you what's in it.**

Homework
- Continue to record the breakthroughs and revelations that you receive in your quiet time with the Father.
- Check the Blog and comment (if one was created).
- Continue journaling daily from His Word.
- Complete the study on God's name, Jehovah-Shalom, The Lord my Peace.

Jehovah-Shalom

Psalm 23:2 *"He maketh me to lie down in green pastures: he leadeth me beside the still waters."*
The Lord is my Peace (Judges 6:24).

Peace is the opposite of strife. *Peace* means "completeness, soundness, or welfare, health."

In what areas do I lack peace?
_____
_____

Who or what steals my peace?
_____
_____

How do I act when I am not at peace?
_____
_____

- Do I take control?
- Do I fly off the handle and vent to alleviate the pressure?
- Do I fall into isolation or self-pity?
- Do I become passive or aggressive?

Isaiah 59:1-8
  Where there are iniquities, there is separation, and it ends with NO PEACE.
  Iniquities are the twisted mindsets we have or our false perceptions of God.
    ** This is why we are going through the God names, to cleanse our perceptions!
  Our iniquities separate us from God.
  The sin (our actions) hides His face from us.

Read Judges 6
Vs. 1—The Israelites did evil in the sight of the Lord, so the Lord *"delivered"* (sold or exchanged) them to the Midianites.
  - Sometimes our trouble is caused by our own doing, from our own stubbornness not to surrender, and not always the devil, although we are QUICK TO BLAME HIM.

Vs. 2—The Midianites started to prevail against the Israelites, so they made dens in the mountains and hid in caves and other strongholds.

When I am faced with losing ground, losing my security, losing my position, losing my control, losing my name or reputation, or losing my image, what is my response?
What is my response when I feel as though I am swimming against the current?

_____
_____
_____

Vs. 7—The children of Israel cried UNTO the Lord BECAUSE OF THE MIDIANITES.
What point do I have to get to before I cry out to the Lord?

_____
_____
_____
_____

Vs. 8-10—The Lord reminded them of everything He had already saved them from and said, *"FEAR NOT."*

FEAR COULD BE A VOICE WE HEED!

2 Timothy 1:7—God has not given us a *"spirit of fear; but of power, and of love and of a sound mind."*
- The voice of Fear we heed is actually a spirit we allow to influence us.
- Fear will give you thoughts and raise your emotions to get you to act on that voice instead of God's voice.
- How does a spirit of fear come at us, and what could the fruit of it look like?
    ° It could come from a root of rejection, which could result in no self-worth or value.
    ° It could come from a root of abandonment, which could result in not letting myself get close to anyone, to protect myself from feeling abandoned.
    ° It could come from low self-esteem, which could result in insecurities rising and me losing my sense of control, which could eventually force me into isolation or false humility.

What are other fruits or thoughts I hear through the "spirit of fear"?

_____
_____

Back to Judges 6:
Vs. 10—"*Fear not the gods of the Amorites ... , but ye have NOT OBEYED my voice.*"

When I look at what I fear or what I am worried about (the fruits of the fear), what does He remind me that I am not doing?

_____
_____
_____
_____

What past victories do I have that I can remind myself of to build my faith now?

_____
_____
_____
_____

To what point or where do I allow fear of _____ to bring me?

_____
_____
_____
_____

Vs. 11—Gideon was hiding behind the winepress to thresh wheat. (We might call him a coward.) Where or how do I hide in my struggle (the darkness) while painting a different picture in reality for others to see?
- Maybe I hide behind excuses.
- Maybe I hide behind pride or false humility, which is the low spectrum of pride.

_____
_____
_____
_____

Vs. 15—Gideon was from the smallest of the Israelite tribes.
There were two half-tribes of Israel, and he was from the smaller half-tribe.

What is the Lord asking me to do or conquer that I "feel" is so small or too big, that it wouldn't even make a difference if I did or didn't do it?

_____
_____
_____
_____

Vs. 22-23—*("And when Gideon perceived that he was an angel of the Lord, Gideon said, Alas, O Lord God! for because I have seen an angel of the Lord face to face. And the Lord said unto him, Peace be unto thee; fear not: thou shalt not die.")* Was Gideon's fear rooted in his perception that because he had seen the angel of the Lord, he would die? The angel of the Lord wanted to comfort him and settle his fears. The angel of the Lord was confronting his fears or the perceptions he had!

Exodus 33:20-23—When the Lord told Moses He would pass by, Moses couldn't see the Lord's face, or he would die.

Exodus 34:5-7—When the Lord passed before Moses

What perception (lie) does the Lord need to root out of me, allowing me to step out and conquer what He's asking me to conquer?

_____
_____
_____
_____

What fears do I need to surrender to the Lord and allow Him to confront so that I can have His peace that's beyond understanding?

_____
_____
_____
_____

Vs. 25-26—Gideon was told to tear down HIS FATHER'S IDOL, an altar to Baal, and build the Lord's altar in its place. You can't have peace if you have idols or walls in the Lord's place!

Notice that what the Lord was asking him to remove wasn't even his, and yet it was affecting him.

What altars, idols, or walls do I have (that didn't necessarily start with me) that I need to tear down and then build an altar to the Lord in their place?

Examples of walls or idols:
- Grudges
- Bitterness
- Vengeance
- Mother-in-law against daughter-in-law
- Accepting abuse
- Being a door mat and being taken advantage of
- Certain belief systems
- Racism
- Being judgmental

_____
_____
_____
_____
_____
_____

Vs. 27—Gideon was being obedient, but he did it at night because of fear of other men and his father's household. He was obeying the Lord his God, but on his own terms.

What do I try to overcome in secret (hoping to privately deal with an area inwardly), all the while hoping that no one finds out I have struggled in that area?

_____
_____
_____
_____

To sum up the chapter, what is the key to how the Israelites opened themselves up for oppression and fear to rise up in them and lost their standing with the Lord, going back into captivity for seven years?

_____
_____
_____
_____

Notice all the times the angel of the Lord confronted Gideon because of his fear of people, because people's opinions, their view of him and what they would say would powerfully influence him. It was in the next chapter that the Lord pruned Gideon's army from 30,000 soldiers to 300. Why? Because the Lord wanted to show Himself strong and for Gideon to no longer surrender to fear through the people, but by Him.

Can you find in Chapter 7 (the next chapter) where the Lord still had to confront Gideon's fear?

Chapter 7

ADAM

Genesis 3:17-19 (AMP)

"Then to Adam the Lord God said, 'Because you have listened [attentively] to the voice of your wife, and have eaten [fruit] from the tree about which I commanded you, saying, "You shall not eat of it"; the ground is [now] under a curse because of you; in sorrow and toil you shall eat [the fruit] of it all the days of your life. Both thorns and thistles it shall grow for you; and you shall eat the plants of the field. By the sweat of your face you will eat bread until you return to the ground, for from it you were taken; for you are dust, and to dust you shall return.'"

And unto Adam he said, because thou hast hearkened unto the voice of thy wife, and hast eaten of the tree of which I commanded thee, saying, Thou shalt not eat of it: cursed is the ground for thy sake.

- *Hearkened* means "hear, listen, or obey."
- *Voice* means "sound, lightness, proclamation."
- *Eaten* means "devour, burn up, feed, consume."
- *Commanded* means "command, promise, intend."
- *Saying* means "to say, speak, utter, to say in one's heart, to think, command, promise, to intend."
- *Cursed* means "to curse, lay under a curse, put a curse on."
- *Ground* means "ground, land, husbandman, husbandry."

Transferred from under _____ to under _____. Romans 6, 7 and 8

This first section is about a transfer of _____ and _____. You can outwardly obey but not inwardly submit. Adam consumed something that was forbidden. He was supposed to attentively listen only to the voice of the Lord God, but he attentively listened to the voice of his wife instead.

87

Maintaining Generational Freedom | 88

Whose voice do you heed over God's?

_____
_____

Matthew 15:1-9
- **Vs. 3**—Jesus asked the scribes and Pharisees, *"Why do ye <u>also transgress</u> the commandment of God by <u>your tradition</u>?"*
  - *Also transgress* means "to overstep, neglect, violate, one who <u>abandons his trust.</u>"
  - *Tradition* means "giving up, giving over, tradition by instruction."
    ° What's our tradition?
    ° An iniquity we (could) inherit is learned behavior of _____. We override God's commandment and His voice because of the iniquity of our trust in Him being abandoned.

- **Vs. 6**—I have made the Word of God of none effect by my _____.
  ° Our culture, family traditions, and lies we believe (of ourselves, others or even God) will cause the Word of God to be ineffective!
  ° Example: If I believe the economy dictates whether or not I get a raise, then my belief takes the power out of God's Word to manifest in my life in that area.
  ° Our beliefs separate us from the LORD our God! These are traditions that are passed down. These are our walls. Through these walls, the enemy comes with "reality" to reinforce the lies we believe, to make sure we don't let our walls down and quit believing his lies.

- **Vs. 8-9**—Our lips draw near to God, but our hearts are far from Him, causing our worship to be ____ _____ because we teach for doctrine *"the commandments ____ _____."* We re-teach from our own walls and through how we see our God and our reality.

Adam could have prevented Eve from being deceived. He knew the truth and had dominion, so could he have avoided all that happened (Numbers 30:1-2, which we will get into later), but didn't? Therefore, we now live under the principle of "we reap what we sow," or you could say, we are being paid according to our actions. Adam was given dominion, power, charge and authority over ALL, but he did not own up to the responsibility he was given or exercise that dominion.

The ground was cursed for Adam's sake (and remained cursed until after the flood). All our work or way of life comes from the ground. We are then paid for our work. This is why _____ BREAKS the curse so the ground would work for us (opening the first river we discussed in Chapter 5).

This is why tithing opens the river:
Genesis 14:18-24
We see that Abram gave the first tithe recorded in the Word.

Genesis 15:1—"*After these things the word of the Lord came to Abram in a vision, saying, 'Fear not Abram: I am thy shield, and thy exceeding great reward.'*"

When Abram honored the Lord through the tithes to the priest Melchizedek, it released certain things in his life:

_____
_____
_____

Man took a step out from under grace and now lived by the law of his members. When we live under legalism, we allow ourselves to be taken back to a prisoner state, negatively affecting the whole family!

In sorrow shalt thou eat of it all the days of thy life.

- *Sorrow* means "pain, labor, hardship, sorrow, toil, worrisome." (from the same root word as "worship, pain, hurt").
- *Eat* means "eat, devour, burn up or feed."
- *All* means "all, the whole, any, each, totality, everything."
- *The days* means "day, time, year, today, yesterday, tomorrow."
- *Life* means "living, alive, relatives, life, community."

Our mindset,

Our _____

Proverbs 18:20

"*A man's belly shall be satisfied with the fruit of his mouth; and with the increase of his lips shall he be filled.*"

- If we are filled by the words that ____ _____, what happens to the words others speak around us that we _____ and don't call down? Do we fill up on those words also?

James 1:12-15

_____
_____
_____
_____
_____

Out of pain, worry, or emotion (whether caused by trauma, disappointment, regrets, etc.), we speak, giving it power to _____ and affect _____ under us! Because the word *days* means "tomorrow," could that be why we have to repent of the sins of our forefathers?

What types of words do you speak that you can see manifesting in your reality?
_____
_____
_____

What types of words do you speak that you can see manifesting in your children's reality?
_____
_____
_____

What types of words did others before you speak that you can see patterns manifesting?
_____
_____
_____

Thorns also thistles shall it bring forth to thee.
- *Thorns* means "sense of pricking" (from a root word meaning "to spend the harvest season").
- *Thistles* is "of uncertain derivation, thorns."

Trials and testing = _____

This follows what you eat. We eat the fruit of what we speak.
Thorns or *thistles* implies "pricking."
Fruit used to come easy. Now he would get fruit through pain.
Of uncertain derivation, meaning "an offense" (which is a twisting).
(Remember the study on Eve)

Think of the first fruit Adam and the woman received after they ate of the tree: _____.

Romans 5:12-20

Vs. 15
- Through the offense of one (Adam), we are _____.
- Through the gift of one (Jesus), we have _____.

Vs. 18
- Through offense, we get a judgment that brings _____, which is a damning sentence.
- Through the free gift (from Jesus), we get _____ of life.

Vs. 19
- Because of one man's disobedience (Adam), we are made _____.
- But by the obedience of one (Jesus), we are made _____.

Matthew 7:15-23
- Warns of false prophets and how to discern them—by their fruit.
- They are false prophets because of the doctrine they live by! It tells us how to check ourselves, our motives, and how to change ourselves.
- All Spirit-filled believers have the simple gift of prophecy and discernment. We all hear God.

What are iniquities again?
_____
_____

What fruit are you producing while in a storm?
Are you speaking from your natural heart (filled with iniquities and hurts), or are you speaking from a heart that has been healed and sees the LORD our God for who He truly is, not just your perception of who He is or is not?
_____
_____
_____
_____

And thou shalt eat the herb of the field
- *Herb* means "to glisten or be green" (Genesis 1:11-12).
- *Field* means "to spread out, field, land, cultivated land, soil."

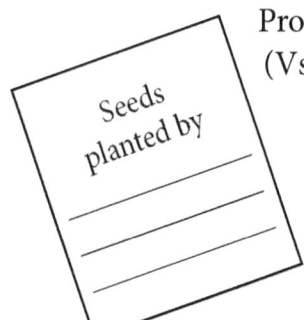

Proverbs 13:2-3

(Vs. 2)—"A man shall eat good by the <u>fruit</u> of his <u>mouth</u>: but the <u>soul</u> of the <u>transgressors</u> shall eat <u>violence</u>."

- *Fruit* means "(literal) of the ground, (of the womb) children, of actions"—**words**.
- *Mouth* means "(literal) mouth, (figurative) speech"—**spoken**.
- *Soul* means "appetite, mind, desire, emotion, passion, heart"—a **vow** (it binds your soul).
- *Transgressors* means "deceitfully, deal or act treacherously, offend"—**made or create**.
- *Violence* means "wrong, cruelty, injustice"—**what we live with**.

To rewrite **Proverbs 13:2-3** with these meanings, it would say:
A man shall eat good by his words spoken, but the vows (that bind his soul) will create what he lives with.

Out of the abundance of our heart, the mouth speaks. Our words are seeds.
We speak or tolerate what others speak over us or our children, and then reap a harvest of fruit from those spoken words later.

What is in your heart becomes your reality!

What seeds are you planting?
_____
_____
_____
_____

What seeds have been planted that need to come up?
_____
_____
_____
_____

What seeds are being planted when we remain silent and tolerate what is being said around us?
_____
_____
_____

What blessings could you be stopping with negative speech?
_____
_____
_____

In the sweat of thy face shalt thou eat bread, till thou return unto the ground; For out of it wast thou taken; for dust thou art, and unto dust shalt thou <u>return</u>.

- *Sweat* means "perspiration," (from a root meaning "to tremble, quiver, quake in terror, to shake off").
- *Face* means "face, anger," (from a root meaning "to be displeased, to breath hard, enraged").
- *Bread* means "fruit or provision."
- *Return* means "to return, turn back, repair, restore."
- *Ground* means "ground, land, soil, husband (husbandman)."
- *Taken* means "to be captured, taken, carried away, seized."
- *Return* means "to return, turn back, to restore, refresh, repair, revoke."

(Malachi 3:7-12—This is why tithes is the first step to breaking the curse! It's the same word *return* as in the end of Adam's judgment!)

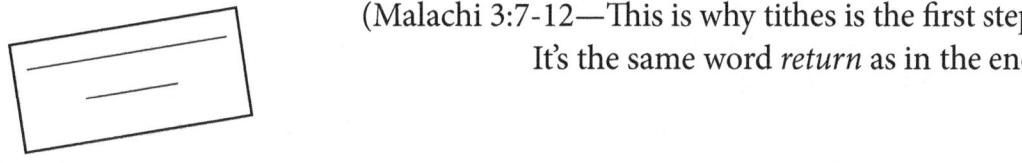

What are we returning?
_____

"In the sweat of thy face" is referring to being in the heat of emotion and speaking things into existence. You and your family will live by the words that were spoken (past), words you speak (present), or words you allow to be spoken over you (future).

Adam and Eve acted out of the offenses formed in them against the Lord God and took of the tree of knowledge, breaking the Lord's commandment (stealing wisdom). Now the steal door was open. They were taken out of the garden so they wouldn't ALSO STEAL from the Tree of Life and live forever. This action broke the covenant of "Everlasting Life," which Jesus, our Savior restored.

Proverbs 1:7—*"The fear of the Lord is the beginning of knowledge: but fools despise wisdom and instruction."*

Maintaining Generational Freedom | 94

Proverbs 1:24-33
- Because I (the LORD) called and you refused —____ ____ ____ ____ ____ ____.
- When _____ _____ comes (vs. 27).
- Then you will call Me, and I will not answer (vs. 28).
- We have to choose the fear of the LORD over our natural fears (vs. 29).
- Because Adam and Eve failed to heed the LORD God and did what they wanted when they wanted, they _____ _____ _____ _____ ____ _____ _____ _____ (the fruit of the flesh) (vs. 31).
- BUT _____ _____ ____ ____ shall dwell safely and be quiet from fear (vs. 33).

Numbers 30:1-2

And Moses spake unto the heads of the tribes concerning the children of Israel, saying, This is the thing which the LORD hath commanded.

- *Spake* means "speak, declare, warn, promise, threaten."
- *Heads* means "head, top, summit, chief, front."
- *Tribes* means "staff, tribe, branch, a company led by a chief."
- *Children* means "son, grandson, a member of a group."
- *Saying* means "to say, speak, utter, to say in one's heart, to think, command, promise, intend."
- *Commanded* means "to command, charge, give orders, lay charge, give charge to, order."

If a man vow a vow unto the LORD, or swear an oath to bind his soul with a bond; he shall not break his word; He shall do according to all that proceedeth out of his mouth.

- *Man* means "male, husband."
- *Vow* means "to vow or make a vow, to promise."
- *Vow* means "vow, votive offering" (from a root meaning the same as the word *vow* above).
- *Swear* means "to swear, adjure, take an oath, to curse, charge."
- *Oath* means "oath, curse" (from a root meaning the same as *swear* above).
- *Bind* means "to tie, bind, to imprison, to be taken prisoner."
- *Soul* means "activity of mind, will or character, appetite."
- *Bond* means "bond, binding obligation" (from a root word meaning "bind").
- *Break* means "to profane, defile, pollute, desecrate, begin, to wound, pierce."
- *Word* means "speech, word, speaking, thing."
- *Do* means "to do, fashion, accomplish, make, produce, maintain."
- *Proceedeth* means "to go out, come out, exit, go forth, depart."
- *Mouth* means "mouth, opening."

Moses was talking to the leaders of the tribes (which is our head of household), concerning their families. He was telling them that IF a man (or a husband) made an ungodly vow or promise unto the Lord or swore, which is to lay oneself under a curse over his soul (binding him), taking him and his family back to a prison state, he would not break his word! Everything he spoke or allowed _____ _____ ____ _____.

Numbers 1:52 (read the whole chapter on your own)

The Israelites had to set their tents according to their _____ _____.
- This whole chapter was addressed to the men of the tribe, heads of households.
- They closed the door or gate to their homes and families based on the conviction level or standard they governed by.

Galatians 6:7-9—God is not mocked. I will reap what I sow and even what I allow others to sow into my life.
"*Whatsoever a man soweth [seed], that shall he also reap [harvest].*"

What is in your heart will **come out your mouth**!

In Adam's heart, there was an offense within himself of the Lord God, which is the ***seed sown.***
Out of his mouth, his first action (he was now under the consequences of his actions) was to rename woman.
- Eve was the second name given to her.

Adam now acted on the seed sown, putting division, or a wall, between himself and Eve, which is **the harvest.**

Genesis 3:21

In the verses following the judgment sentenced, what was the Lord God's first action to atone Adam and woman back to Himself?

_____
_____
_____

Through the use of animal skins (blood sacrifice), the Lord God atoned for them. Their acceptance of the Lord God's covering was the way of covering their sin. The Lord God showed us why He used an animal skin to cover them. It was symbolic of what was to come.

> **Leviticus 17:11**—The blood makes an atonement for our sin.
> **Hebrews 9:18-22**—Without shedding of blood there is no forgiveness of sin.

River #1 may be closed off because of the offense, or separation, we inherited and are living under (the consequence spoken to Adam).
- The ground was cursed but still worked for them because their sin was forgiven.
- We have to return our trust back to God through tithes (a symbolic gesture, not to be done reluctantly). River #1 – Increase
- Adam's position before the fall:
    - He had dominion and could have told the serpent to stop talking. He failed to use his voice and, instead, took lightly his communion with the Lord God. Instead of asking the Lord God if He was holding out wisdom (as he was led by Satan through the influence of another—woman), it caused Adam to question his loyalty. By allowing this accusation against the Lord God to become his truth of who He was, Adam let pride set in and "messed up" his easy communication with the Lord God.
    - He failed to govern though his authority to stop woman's soul from being vexed (Numbers 30). He was passive.
- Living under Adam's judgment can bring us back to a prisoner state. The end of his judgment talks about binding his soul (being imprisoned). Only true forgiveness takes you out of prison.
- **A man is saved (*sozo'd*), which is complete healing through his knowledge of God, not referring to salvation (see 1 Timothy 2:4).**

River #2 may be closed off because we are living under the consequence spoken to Eve.
- The multiplication of sorrow and conception, and in sorrow bringing forth children (the learned behavior key).
- With Eve, it was a daily sanctification. We have to crucify the flesh, reigning in our own emotions! When we hit a wall, we have to hit it head on and BURST through it, to prevent us from detouring and going around that wall. The Lord God wants us to turn to Him and not take from the tree of knowledge daily within ourselves. River #2 — Bursting Forth
- Living under Eve's consequences would bring us back to a captive state. This was her struggle: her consequences were in her emotions being multiplied to the point of worshipping them. Thus, she was held captive within herself.
- Her emotions were tested. Will we heed the Holy Spirit, taking us out of captivity, or fail to heed the Holy Spirit, leading us back into captivity?
- **A woman is saved (*sozo'd*), which is complete healing, through childbearing and performing her parental duties (see 1 Timothy 2:15).**

Under the Tree of Knowledge
- "God's tithe"
- A test of loyalty and trust
    - God's way to redeem the land
    - The tree of knowledge represented the test of true devotion, trust and loyalty, leaning on the Lord God for all wisdom and knowledge.
    - They took of it instead of asking the Lord God for wisdom.

Homework
- Continue keeping a list of the breakthrough and revelations as you start to receive them in your daily quiet time with the Father.
- Check the Blog and comment (if one was created).
- Continue journaling daily from His Word.
- Complete the Definition Sheet and Reference Scriptures that follow.

DEFINITIONS

Define these words using *Webster's* or a good online dictionary. Do your best to find Bible references in which the word or the meaning of the word is used. Then define the words from a biblical point of view (referring to a good Bible dictionary).

STUBBORN
Webster's: _____
_____
_____

Bible References: _____
_____
_____

Biblical Meaning: _____
_____
_____

REBELLION
Webster's: _____
_____
_____

Bible References: _____
_____
_____

Biblical Meaning: _____
_____
_____

SACRIFICE
Webster's: _____
_____
_____

Bible References: _____
_____
_____

Biblical Meaning: _____
_____
_____

CONSCIOUS
Webster's: _____
_____
_____

Bible References: _____
_____
_____

Biblical Meaning: _____
_____
_____

CONSCIENCE
Webster's: _____
_____
_____

Bible References: _____
_____
_____

Biblical Meaning: _____
_____
_____

Reference Scriptures

Hosea 10:8—*"The <u>high place</u> also of <u>Aven</u>, the <u>sin</u> of Israel, shall be destroyed: the thorn and the thistle shall come upon their altars; and they shall say to the mountains, <u>Cover</u> us; and to the hills, Fall on us."*

Think of our armor and spiritual warfare (2 Corinthians 10:4-5).
Our armor is for the pulling down of strongholds and imaginations (the high places in us).
- *High places* means "high or elevation."
- *Aven* means "vanity, places for idolatrous worship" (from a root word meaning "trouble, wickedness, sorrow, idolatry").
- *Sin* means "sin, punishment, an offense (sometimes habitual)."
- *Cover* means "cover, conceal, hide, overwhelm."
      **** (*Thorn* or *thistle* here is the same word as in Adam's judgment).

The "high places" were the most important sin of Israel. High places that must be destroyed are the "elevated idols" in our heart that we want to hide. High places in our hearts that we want to hide and keep are the "thorns and thistles."

What thorns or thistles (irritations, thoughts, judgments, and reactions) do I have that I want to keep and hide?
What rubs me wrong?
What insecurities do I harbor that I am hiding from others?
Example: Pride | Trust issues | Rejection | Suppressed Anger | Resentment

_____
_____
_____
_____
_____
_____
_____
_____

Matthew 13:10-23

This is the Parable of the Four Soils.

What are the four conditions of my heart that the Word of God can fall on? And what is significant about each of them?

#1— _____

#2— _____

#3— _____

#4— _____

Which of these four conditions do I think my heart is currently in and why?
(Hint: I can be in different levels of different conditions in different circumstances at the same time.)

Matthew 7:15-20
- *False prophet* here can be defined as a sheep on the outside, a wolf on the inside, a HYPOCRITE. On the outside (what people see), they speak the Word and participate in church life, but inside (what no one sees), they are wrapped up in thorns and thistles (demonic battles and strongholds such as bitterness, rejection, insecurity, feeling unloved, unwanted, etc).
- It tells us to know a prophet by their fruit!
  (Good trees can't bear bad fruit, and bad trees can't bear good fruit.)
- You produce fruit according to the doctrine you live by! A seed produces after its own kind. Galatians 6:7—*"God is not mocked: for whatsoever a man soweth, that shall he also reap."*

Two thoughts:

- In what areas do I say one thing (speak the Word or follow the crowd), but inwardly I am fighting a very different battle?

  _____
  _____
  _____
  _____
  _____
  _____
  _____

- What patterns or habits (good or bad) do I have that my children or others are receiving, with the opportunity to pass them on down to others?

  _____
  _____
  _____
  _____
  _____
  _____
  _____

Chapter 8

Introduction to the "Kill" Door

This door is mainly opened and closed by "_____ _____."

This manifests in the physical (sickness, spiritual idolatry, reality, our bodies, hornets).
To fully understand learned behavior, look at the children of Israel as they left Egypt for the Promised Land.

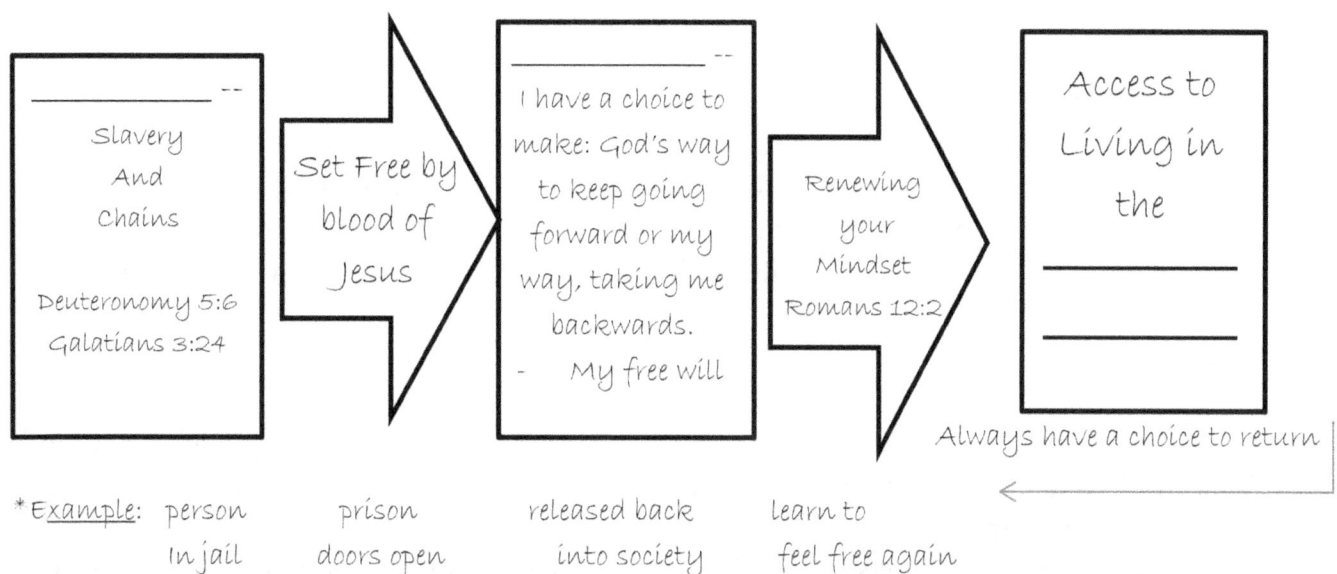

****NONE of these stages means that I am referring to someone not being saved!

How does this relate to our spiritual walk and the doors?
- If we are not teachable, we return to our bondage (_____).

This door is learned behavior and allowing the Holy Spirit ____ _____ _____ His way.
- Titus 3:1-7
    Vs. 5—"According to His mercy He saved us THROUGH the washing of the regeneration and renewing of the Spirit."

- Matthew 19:23-30
  Vs. 28—(words of Jesus) *"Ye which have followed me in the regeneration"*

We have to be willing to be teachable by the Holy Spirit, allowing Him to renew our minds, changing how we perceive, see and learn, to **maintain** and **walk** in the freedom bought by Christ on the cross.

Explanation:
- If we are wrapped in bondage (sin, porn, anger, rejection, low self-worth), this is our "_____."
- When we get saved, everything is done. We are free. It is all nailed to the cross.
- We are now in the wilderness part of our journey, the testing season, the purification process.
- We can choose the Lord's way and not our own _____ _____ (which is spiritual idolatry, our wounds that scream at us that we knew from Egypt, our learned behavior and habits).
- We can complain and want to go back to Egypt because it is more familiar.
- We can continue circling the same mountain over and over again, at times because we trust our pain and hurts, so we justify why we are staying the way we are, or we can push through to the other side.
- We have a choice to make to change how we _____ _____ _____ things, renewing our mind in the Word and changing our behavior.
- Through the leading of the Holy Spirit, we now have opportunity to experience the Promised Land, and with a renewed mind, we can maintain it by pulling down everything that rises against the Word of God. (This works only if you know the Word for yourself and not someone else's version of the Word.)

Iniquity—(Webster's) "Gross injustice or wickedness. A violation of right or duty, wicked act, sin."
  (Biblical)—"Guilt of iniquity, punishment of iniquity … not the action, but the character of the action, the consequence" (Exodus 20:5).
  <u>Examples</u>—The roots of our actions, such as bitterness, rejection, resentment, pride, jealousy, anger, and failure.

At times, our identity or how we label people _____ _____ _____.
<u>Example</u>—Our Identity becomes "hot head" to cover an anger root.

Offense—(Webster's) "A cause of transgression or the wrong, something that offends or displeases, act of offending or displeasing, the feeling of resentful displeasure caused."
  (Biblical)—"To fall beside or near something, a lapse or deviation from truth and uprightness, to turn aside, wander" (Romans 5:17-20).

Introduction to the "Kill" Door | 105

Examples—To self-protect, building walls or reasons to avoid someone or something. It could appear as _____ to cover a wound.

Self-promotion: To build ourselves up (I did a good job). This could appear as _____ to cover a wound of _____ _____-_____.

Self-rejection: Making a joke and, thus, rejecting myself before someone else does it, to cover _____ .

When _____ (roots) rise, an _____ (a transgression that leads to an action) will usually come to _____ or _____ the iniquity.

WHAT THE DOOR LOOKS LIKE:
I referred to it looking like _____ _____ .

Deuteronomy 5:6-21
- Vs. 6—"*The LORD thy God brought us out of Egypt, a house of _____.*"
- Vs. 7-21—The 10 Commandments
  Commandment #4 – To keep the Sabbath Holy…

Why is this important?

_____
_____
_____
_____
_____
_____
_____

Galatians 3:23-24
- Before faith, we were under the Law (_____ _____).
- The Law was our schoolmaster (_____) to bring us to Christ.
- The commandments are a _____ and a _____ to keep us headed toward the Promised Land and not going back to Egypt (see Galatians 3:15-18).

Maintaining Generational Freedom | 106

HOW DO WE WORK ON CLOSING THE DOOR?
Closing the door comes with a new _____ and a different _____ .

Hebrews 12:2-24 (READ AND FOCUS ON VERSE 14-17 FOR THE CHART)
Three things God warns us to watch for:

*** Could they go with what helps to open the three doors?

	STEAL	KILL	DESTROY
The warnings:			
How to check myself?			
Where does the enemy attack me?			
What does it look like?			

How do you know if you are passing the iniquity?

HOW TO MAINTAIN THE DOOR CLOSED:

We can refrain from reopening the door by understanding what a hornet is, as the Holy Spirit reveals it to us. As we endure a trial, choosing loyalty and sincere trust in God only, we pass the test. (James 1:12).

Deuteronomy 7:12-20

_____
_____
_____
_____
_____
_____
_____

Hebrews 10:35-39
If we pass the test and do the _____ ____ _____, we may receive the promise.

_____
_____
_____
_____
_____
_____
_____

- Continue keeping a list of the breakthroughs and revelations you receive in your quiet time with the Father.
- Check the Blog and comment (if one was created).
- Continue journaling daily from His Word.
- Complete the study on the God name Jehovah-Rophi, The Lord our Healer, that follows.

JEHOVAH-ROPHI

Psalm 23:3(a) *"He restoreth my soul."*
The Lord is my Health, Healing Physician (Exodus 15:26).

What area am I believing the Lord to restore or heal?
Family? Friends? Relationship with children or parents? Sickness or disease? Allergies? Anxieties?

_____
_____
_____

Read Exodus 15:22-26
Vs. 22—The wilderness, the state of figuring out what's happening
    They were looking for water.
What water am I looking for?
What refreshes me, helping to take the edge off?

_____
_____
_____
_____
_____
_____

Vs. 23—*Marah* represents "bitterness."
Bitterness is what "sprung up" in Cain (see Hebrews 12).
Bitterness is the start of a wound (a perception of something that happened or something I wanted to
    happen that didn't) that separates me from the Lord my God.
When we hold bitterness against someone in the physical, it affects our relationship with the Lord.
    A Father Wound in the physical affects how you look at Father God.
    A Mother Wound in the physical affects how you look at the Holy Spirit.
    A Sibling or Friend Wound in the physical affects how you look at Jesus.

Examples:
> If you've had an abusive, neglectful or absent dad or other authority figure on Earth, you may think God will take advantage of you. This affects your relationship with the Father.
>
> If your mother or a mother figure in your life was manipulative, controlling or co-dependent to get her way, then you may feel as though the Holy Spirit will trick you or want to control you. This affects your relationship with the Holy Spirit.
>
> If you told a friend a secret and were betrayed, then you may not trust the Lord to come into the deep parts of your heart because what if He leaves you or puts you in a corner and isn't there for you or doesn't come through for you. This affects your relationship with the Son, Jesus.

There are three things that occur which can cause us to become bitter and create our identity.
1. Something was withheld from us or never given through circumstances or choice.
   > Example: You only had one parent and never felt love, value, or respect.
2. Something was given but then taken away, and this created trauma in you.
   > Example: A parent died early in your life, you were raped, or through incest, you lost your virginity and self-respect, or you lost a close friend.
3. Maybe you feel cheated of something.
   > Example: Love, acceptance, freedom, or perhaps molestation you suffered, or a dysfunctional family or bullying cheated you out of a healthy childhood.)

** If you allow bitterness to take root, you, in turn, start opening the doors.**

When reading the above list and examples, which one triggers an emotion in me?

_____
_____
_____

Is the person who triggered the emotion in me linked to what I want healed? If so, why do I think this is true?

_____
_____
_____
_____
_____
_____

Vs. 25—When Moses called out to the Lord, the Lord showed him a tree, and he put it in the water, transforming the water from bitter to sweet.

The tree is symbolic of the cross!

When Jesus is put into the middle of my circumstance, He transforms it.

What area or situation do I need Jesus to transform and heal?

_____
_____
_____
_____
_____
_____
_____

Once the water was transformed (made sweet), the Lord made a statue (limit or boundary) and an ordinance (judgment, privilege, manner, plan), and there He proved (test, try, or prove) them.

What limits or privileges do I receive as a test to see if I will uphold my end of the agreement with the Lord?

We say "Lord, if You do _____, then I will _____."

This is a covenant!

Do I keep my covenant, or do I take it lightly and go back on it?

_____
_____
_____
_____
_____
_____
_____

Vs. 26—We see the word "IF."

If means that the second part of what I'm saying is based on the first part being completed.

"IF" you:
- Diligently listen (Adam didn't listen only to the Lord God).
- Do what's right (Cain didn't do what was right and accepted).
- Give ear to the commandments (Esau listened to his perception, his wound, and sold his birthright for a morsel of food).
- Keep all My statutes (listen and obey).

I WILL PUT NONE OF THESE DISEASES UPON THEE.

Look at the areas you listed above that you want the Lord to heal or restore.
Are you willing to put the Lord in the middle of them and do what He says?
Even if it means forgiving yourself?

Once I get my healing, will I listen to what the Lord is telling me, or do I think I can maintain my healing on my own?

_____
_____
_____
_____
_____
_____
_____

If I think it's within my power to fix a situation, do I even bother to put the Lord in the middle of it?

_____
_____
_____
_____
_____
_____
_____

Because I am determined to do things my way, what sicknesses, hornets, or situations do I wrestle with due to disobedience or rebellion toward the Lord God?

_____
_____
_____
_____
_____
_____
_____

Do I lean on my own knowledge or that of doctors and only go to the Lord God when things look incurable?

_____
_____
_____
_____
_____
_____
_____

Chapter 9

Cain and Abel

Genesis 4:1-7

"Cain was a tiller of the ground" (physical).
We have to till the ground of our heart (spiritual).

- Vs. 5—Cain and his offering were not respected.

Why?

_____
_____
_____
_____

Hebrews 11:4—" _____ _____ , Abel offered unto God a more excellent sacrifice than Cain."
Faith here, in the original meaning, refers to a _____ ____ _____.

What is faith?

_____
_____
_____
_____

According to Hebrews: Cain's offering was not given in faith. Was it because of something on the _____ _____ _____ that it was not respected?

James 2:14-26 – *"Faith [the conviction of truth] without works [deed, labor, act] is _____."*

113

- Genesis 4:6—The Lord addressed Cain's anger.

Why did Cain get angry?

_____
_____
_____
_____

What are the dangers of an undealt-with offense?

_____
_____
_____
_____

1 John 3:9-18
- Vs. 12—Cain's actions were of the evil one. Notice that he killed because his brother's actions were more righteous, while his were evil. If you let the sun go down on your wrath, you give a foothold to Satan.
- Vs. 15—If you hate your brother, you are a murderer.
- Vs. 17—If you see a need and do nothing about it …
- Vs. 18—Love is expressed in your actions and lifestyle, not just your speech.

How do we fall into this same category and murder someone and walk away, feeling justified and leaving them to bleed?

_____
_____
_____
_____

1 John 4:1
- "_____ _____ *every spirit.*"
  The emotion rising in Cain could have been a hornet,
  showing him something was there that had not been dealt with.

1 John 4:20
- If you cannot love your brother whom you see, you don't love God whom you don't see.
- This is the _____, whatever is going on with people will affect your relationship with the Lord God.

Cain and Abel | 115

Matthew 5:21-26 (words of Jesus, His teaching about anger)
- Refers to the commandment, *"Thou shall not kill."*
- If you are angry with your brother _____ __ _____, you are in danger of judgment (a punishment issued by a court).
- What do you think *"without a cause"* would mean?

_____
_____
_____
_____
_____

  ◦ This is an inward way of breaking this commandment.
  ◦ Is this possibly where Cain was because his brother's offering was accepted and not his own?

- If you at the altar and there remember our brother has something against you, leave your gift at the altar and go reconcile with him. Then come back to offer your gift to your Father in Heaven.
  ◦ We are given the ministry of _____.

- *"Agree with thine adversary quickly…"*
  ◦ When you make a mental decision to do something, do it quickly. Why?

What's the enemy's first tactic against us?
_____

If you allow doubt to have its way within you and you don't reconcile, while you are on your way, he (the adversary) will deliver you to the judge, then to the officer, and you can end up in prison with undealt-with emotions.

The way it possibly happens in our mind:
◦ We make a mental decision to do what the Holy Spirit is laying on our heart to do.
◦ Once our emotions subside and life goes on, our mind plays with us and tells us that it doesn't matter if we do it or not. We tend not to see what difference it would make, so we change our mind and don't do it. Instead, we can suppress our emotions, holding on to the unforgiveness, grudge, resentment, etc.
◦ Now we are in open rebellion with the Holy Spirit, rejecting His direction and openly refusing to heed His voice. This open rebellion and our refusal then lead us into sin.
  * If we choose to be soul-led by the deception and allow the doubt to continually have a place within us, Satan has just changed our direction and focus (_____ _____), and now has an opportunity to steal from us again.
◦ Our choices place us under the enemy's control. Because of our rebellion, God hands us over to the power of condemnation (guilt and shame). Then condemnation will hand us

Maintaining Generational Freedom | 116

over as a slave (acting on those feelings and thoughts, the iniquities), and we will be back in prison and isolation.

We have to choose to deal with the emotions that arise as they arise. If left _____ through rejecting the Lord God in rebellion, we open the door (_____) for Satan to work in our lives. We have a choice, to control the emotions, or allow the emotions and the mindset to control us, placing us under a curse in which we do that which we don't want to do and don't do what we want to do, as Paul said in Romans!

> **Genesis 4:7—*"If thou [you] doest well, shalt thou not be accepted?***
> ***and if thou [you] doest not well, sin lieth at the door.***
> ***And unto thee [you] shall be his [sin's] desire,***
> ***and thou [sin] shalt rule over him [you]."***

The Lord was trying to reassure him ____ _____ _____ what was in his heart, to do what was right!
Don't give Satan any ground in your heart.
Come clean and do what's right, or sin lies at the door waiting for you.

Genesis 4:8-10
Vs. 8—*"It came to pass…"*
- Over a period of time, because it was _____ and not dealt with, his anger started to _____ _____ _____ ; he became a slave to his emotions.
- He now acted on his emotions (a transgression).
- This is the opportunity to sin that lay at the door. The Lord wanted Cain to deal with his emotions because undealt-with emotions become suppressed emotions.

Vs. 9—The Lord asked Cain, *"Where is Abel thy brother?"*
- The Lord gave Cain an _____ _____, just as He did with Adam and Eve!

Vs.10—The Lord confronted what Cain did. He wanted the iniquity out of Cain.

What COULD HAVE BEEN the iniquity, the offense, the Lord wanted to purge out of Cain?
_____
_____
_____
_____

CAIN'S CURSE

Genesis 4:11-12

And NOW art thou cursed From the earth, which hath opened her mouth to receive thy brother's blood from thy hand.
- *Earth* means "ground, land, territory, city in Naphtali."
- *Opened* means "to separate, part, open."
- *Hand* means "hand, strength, power, support."

With Adam, the Lord said, *"Cursed is the ground for your sake."*
With Cain, the Lord said, *"NOW, you [Cain] are cursed from the earth."*
Through Cain's continual rebellion against the Lord and his refusal to deal with himself, he, by his own actions, _____ _____ under a curse.

When thou tillest the ground, it shall not henceforth yield unto thee her strength.
- *Tillest* means "work, serve; serve, work, worshipper."
- *Ground* means "ground, land, territory, city of Naphtali."
- *Henceforth* means "add, increase, do again, continue, give."
- *Strength* means "strength, power, might, human strength, strength of angels, power of God, produce, wealth, ability, fruits."

- MAYBE when the Lord God performed the first blood sacrifice, covering Adam and Eve with the animal skin, the sin was atoned for, leaving mercy and grace to cover their future actions. Therefore, the ground worked for them, but the land was still cursed.
- When we work (out of our own strength), worship or serve the ground or the life we live (making it an idol), it WILL NOT add, increase, or give us strength, wealth, ability, or fruits (see Jeremiah 17:5).
- *Her strength* is referring to the ground's strength.
- If we are working in protection and work mode, where we have to protect ourselves rather than allowing the Lord God to be our Protector, we WILL NOT have the strength or power of the Holy Spirit because we are acting as our own god.

Idol means "image."   *Idolatry* means "worshipping that image."

- *Image* is the root word of *imagination*. If you think on something more than the Lord God, it can possibly become _____ _____ in your heart.

Maintaining Generational Freedom | 118

1 Corinthians 5:1-8
- Vs. 5—Because of the fornication (harlotry, idolatry), you are delivered to Satan for the _____ ____ _____ _____.
- Vs. 6-8—Purge yourself of the leaven.
  ○ A little leaven destroys the whole batch.

What could be the leaven we are to get rid of in our hearts?

_____
_____
_____
_____

James 5:15-16 — A two-step process
- First step (in verse 15)—_____ _____ _____ (what you believe) saves the sick and sins are forgiven.
- Second step (in verse 16)—_____ can bring our healing; we have to expose our thoughts, battles, feelings, and breakthroughs. What we overcome, by finding the truth, becomes our testimony.

A fugitive and a vagabond shalt thou be in the earth.

- *Fugitive* means "quiver, totter, shake, stagger, wander, wave, tossed back and around."
- *Vagabond* means "shake, wander, move to and fro, flutter, show grief."
- *Earth* means "land (inhabitants of the land), earth, wilderness."

If you live under your own wisdom (your truth, pride, or false humility), becoming your own god, you will be tossed back and forth with the wind. You will doubt yourself, doubt others, and maybe even doubt the Lord God. You won't have any sure foundation in the truth.

The misplaced truth, which is the offense, will lead to fear. When a situation arises, fear will grip you instead of God's peace.

Ephesians 4:14
- Children are tossed back and forth and carried with every wind of doctrine.
- Heart immaturity in the Lord will cause us to sway back and forth through the influence of others.

Genesis 4:13-14

*"And Cain said unto the L*ORD*, my punishment [iniquity, guilt] is greater than I can bear [lift up, carry, take, endure]."*

Behold, thou hast driven me out this day from the face of the earth; and from thy face shall I be hid.

- *Driven* means "to drive out, expel, cast out, divorce, put away."
- *Face* means "face, presence."
- *Earth* means "ground, land, territory, city of Naphtali."
- *Hid* means "to hide, conceal, secret, by covering, be absent."

And I shall be a fugitive and a vagabond in the earth; and it shall come to pass, that everyone that findeth me shall slay me.

- *Earth* means "land (inhabitants of the land), earth, wilderness."
- *Come to pass* means "to become, exist, happen, fall out."
- *Slay* means "to kill, murder, destroy, out of hand."

Notice, he _____ _____ _____ for driving him out.
- The LORD God doesn't leave us, but we leave Him.
  ○ **Isaiah 59:2**—Our iniquities separate us from God.
  ○ **Hebrews 13:5**—The LORD says He will *"never"* leave us *"nor"* forsake us.
- Cain went out from the LORD's presence because he wasn't willing to deal with himself.
- Cain went on to tell the LORD his own punishment. (Could this have been a judgment upon himself?)
- We do eat the fruit of our lips, and Cain spoke out his own punishment and how others would treat him.

What do we pronounce as our own reality or the reality over our children?

_____
_____
_____
_____

Cain was worried about _____. He was now carrying his undealt-with offenses against the LORD God and also man (Abel). He was self-protecting and self-seeking. He was now _____ the LORD that the punishment would be too hard to bear.

Maintaining Generational Freedom | 120

1 Corinthians 10:13
> *"There hath no temptation taken you but such as is common to man: but God is faithful, who will not suffer you to be tempted above that ye are able; but will with the temptation also make a way to escape, that ye may be able to bear it."*

Do we do this same thing, blaming the Lord that He is giving us more than we can handle or more than we deserve, not clearly seeing the whole picture?

_____
_____
_____
_____

Cain was telling the Lord that the consequences of his sin were too much. He would no longer be in the Lord's presence. He would have a covering (or veil) that prevented him from seeing the Lord. He would now be unstable, tossed back and forth. From then on, anyone who met him would want to destroy (murder) him (because he murdered Abel). He was afraid to reap what he had sowed! His iniquity was following him.

Notice: NOT ONCE did he _____, admit his _____, or take _____ for his actions, doing the same as Adam had.

Vs. 15—The Lord marked Cain as a sign to everyone not to kill him.

Vs. 16—Adam and Eve were driven out of the Garden of Eden, but they still remained in the city of Eden.
Cain went out from the (manifest) presence of the Lord (not the omnipresence or all-seeing presence of the Lord) and from Eden, dwelling in the land of Nod on the east side of Eden.

Hebrews 10:26—*"If we sin willfully after that we have received _____ _____ of the truth, there remaineth no more sacrifice for sins."*

A Fugitive Spirit
Scriptures the original word is found in and the meanings

Biblical Meaning—"quiver, totter, shake, stagger, wander, wave, tossed back and around"
Webster's Meanaing—"a person who is fleeing from prosecution, runaway, wandering, roving"

James 1:1-8
Vs. 5-8—*"If any of you lack wisdom, let him ask [don't do like Adam and take] of God that giveth to all men liberally [openly], and upbraideth not [without reproach or shame]; and it shall be given him. But let him ask in faith [believing he will get it], nothing WAVERING. For he that <u>wavereth</u> [doubts] is like a wave of the sea driven with the wind and tossed. For let not that man [the one wavering] think that he shall receive any thing of the Lord. A double minded [doubting, divided in interest] man is unstable [inconstant, restless] in all his ways [thinking, feeling, deciding]."*

Psalm 107:27—*"They reel <u>to and fro</u>, and stagger like a drunken man, and are at wits' end."*

Jeremiah 14:10—*"Thus saith the* Lord *unto his people, Thus have they loved <u>to wander</u>, they have not refrained their feet, THEREFORE THE LORD DOTH NOT accept them; he **will now remember their iniquity and visit their sins.**"*

A fugitive spirit is someone who changes their mind when the wind changes direction or when an offense comes. They may agree to do something to make you happy, but when testing and tribulation come, they change _____ _____ to everyone they are around because their life is not built upon solid doctrine. Do you always look over your shoulder, expecting to be stabbed in the back, so that you stay on the defensive and self-protect? What are your survival responses?

A Vagabond Spirit
Scriptures the original word is found in and the meaning.

Biblical Meaning—"shake, wander, move to and fro, flutter, show grief"
Webster's Meaning—"wandering from place to place without any settled home, leading an unsettled, carefree life, having an uncertain or irregular course or direction, a person without a permanent home, an irresponsible person"

Psalm 69:20—*"Reproach [shame] hath broken my heart; and I am full of heaviness [to be sick]: and I looked for some to take <u>pity</u> [waver, show grief], but there was none; and for comforters, but I found none."*

A vagabond spirit opens the door to _____ (Psalm 69). It also causes you to **not** know or misuse your authority and power as king. Because you are **not** living life the way you were created to live it, some seem to have a deep void from within that causes them to pursue people's pity, live in co-dependency, or constantly need the approval of others. They want validation from _____ instead of the Lord God. A vagabond can be easily _____ and doesn't have _____ _____.

1 Samuel 15:22-23—*"And Samuel said, Hath the Lord as great delight in burnt offerings and sacrifices, as in obeying the voice of the Lord? Behold, to obey is better than sacrifice, and to hearken than the fat of rams. For rebellion is as the sin of witchcraft, and stubbornness is as iniquity and idolatry. Because thou hast rejected the word of the Lord, he hath also rejected thee from being king."*

To rewrite the scripture with the words we use today, this might say:

"For rebellion [resisting the Lord's order of authority, which comes from bitterness] is as the sin of witchcraft [manipulation and divination], and stubbornness [which could be in the form of disobedience, self-will, presumption, arrogance, defiance, or pride] is as iniquity [root cause, a way of seeing things] and idolatry [a family idol, unfaithfulness]."

Why is obedience better than sacrifice and to hearken than the fat of rams?

_____
_____
_____
_____

- Doing things Cain's way, with an undealt-with offense, the offering COULD BE offered out of the same iniquity or ignored offense as Adam had, resulting in him covering their shame and condemnation himself, his own way.
- It is different in the physical but the same in the spiritual!
- If you reject the Word of the Lord, the Lord rejects (or refuses) you to be king.

**YOU DON'T GET THE POWER YOU WANT TO TELL
THE MOUNTAIN TO MOVE AND SEE IT MOVE!**

Romans 5:17—*"For if by one man's offence death reigned by one; much more they which receive abundance of grace and the of the gift of righteousness shall reign in life by one, Jesus Christ."*

Romans 5:20—*"Moreover the law entered [came in secretly], that the offence [deviation of the truth] might abound [to exist in abundance]. But where sin abounded, grace did much more abound."*

- The law entered with Adam, when he believed that the Lord God was holding out on him and acted through disobedience. Through Adam's transgression, he became his own god and took wisdom he did not believe he was getting from the Lord.

*** I call this the intrusion that led him to believe a lie, which started a stronghold within him. ***

- Because of Adam's offense with the LORD God, the belief Adam held had opportunity to exist in abundance with Cain.
- The offense is within us, and it draws us to partake of the tree of the knowledge of good and evil. But whatever is in us, <u>WILL</u> manifest in the physical.

Adam felt the rejection (spiritual), but he didn't live it.
Cain lived the rejection (physically), allowing it to become his reality!

*****<u>What's in the HEART of one generation is in the HAND of another!</u>*****

** See also Isaiah 65:6-7

The LORD doesn't leave us! He didn't leave Adam or Cain, but our rebellion and stubbornness, even to ourselves, can bring us to a place where we leave the LORD's presence and find ourselves feeling justified and operating in our own strength and power and under our own protection and provision, placing our trust and loyalty on that instead of on the LORD, which becomes our idolatry.

Homework
- Continue to record breakthroughs and revelations as you receive them in your quiet time with the Father.
- Check the Blog and comment (if one was created).
- Continue journaling daily from His Word.
- Complete the chart that follows with your revelation as you read the suggested passages.
- Complete the study on the God name Jehovah-Tsidkenu, The LORD our Righteousness.

FILL IN THE FOLLLOWING CHART TO THE BEST OF YOUR ABILITY:

Matthew 5:21-26 (The process of anger)	James 1:13-15 (The process of how sin grows)	Cain's choice Genesis 4:4-8 (Cain's actions)	The Consequence Genesis 4:9-16 (The LORD dealing with Cain)
1. A chance to be _____ (Change your mindset, to repent)	1. Tempted with _____ (to follow what he perceived by how he saw) (A desire, a draw or pull, longing for what's forbidden, an emotion)	1. (vs. 4) Cain's offering _____ (Hebrews 11:4 because it was not of faith)	1. The LORD -- Where's _____? (Chance of repentance/ open door)
2. Delivered to _____ (May start to feel condemnation)	2. _____ to do his will instead of God's (Bait, metaphorically deceive) -Tempted to be his own strength, which was his own wisdom	2. (vs. 6) He is _____ (His face was downcast, his body language changed.)	2. Cain -- "Am I my _____?" (He felt guilt, condemnation, but he avoided blame.) - He was feeling justified. -He suppressed his emotions.
3. Delivered to _____ (Assistant)	3. _____ conceived, brings sin (sin: an offense, wandering from the Law of God)	3. (Vs. 8) talked and _____ (He didn't deal with his anger but suppressed it, letting it grow.) - Eat the fruit of your lips.	3. The LORD _____ what he did… "The blood cries out." (Things are brought into the light and exposed.)
4. Cast _____ _____ (Isolation, separation) -Prison takes more than just you.	4. _____ full grown brings _____. (Root – to be spiritually dead)	4. (Vs. 8) attacked and _____ Abel. (Murder, now he is sentenced.)	4. NOW YOU ARE _____ from the Earth and _____ (We have a veil over our face, and the secret things of God are hidden.)

JEHOVAH–TSIDKENU

Psalm 23:3 *"He leadeth me in the paths of righteousness for his name's sake."*
The LORD is my Righteousness (Jeremiah 23:6).

Define these terms:

Righteousness: _____
_____
_____

Self-Righteous: _____
_____
_____

Jeremiah 23:1-8
- This pastor leads his flock wrongly (vs. 1).
- And he reaps HIS OWN evil doing (vs. 2).
- The LORD Himself gathers the flock together and directs them to true shepherds (vs. 3-4).

Pastor means "to pasture, tend, graze, feed, to associate with, be a friend of."
We are all pastors of a sort!
Here he was talking to the pastor who destroys and scatters the sheep of HIS pasture.
A pastor will lead and feed people.
    <u>Examples</u>: A Bible study, fellowship. As parents, we pastor our own homes.

Jeremiah 23:9-40
- This passage describes a false prophet and priest and how we do the same unknowingly.
- They speak visions of their own heart (vs. 16).
- They say peace and no evil will come to those who walk after the imagination of their own heart (vs. 17).
- As an example, we can simply do this unknowingly by teaching others to self-protect the way we self-protect because we haven't yet been delivered from the effects of betrayal.

Maintaining Generational Freedom | 126

How or in what areas can I do this unknowingly?

_____
_____
_____
_____

As a father, mother, husband or wife, do I lead my home?
Do I lead my spouse or try to rule instead?
Am I active or passive in my daily life?
Do I lead my children by a set standard? Or do I allow school, friends, daycare workers, babysitters, or the TV to set a standard for them?
Do I interact with my children? Or do I leave that to their teachers or youth leaders?

_____
_____
_____
_____
_____
_____

When I think of the people I have influence over, do I scatter them blindly through division, still operating through my undealt-with wounds or my perceptions that are then passed down to my children?
Notice, in Jeremiah 23:34, the Lord punished *"THAT MAN AND HIS HOUSE."*

_____
_____
_____
_____
_____
_____

Matthew 15:14
- Are you the blind leading the blind?
- Do YOU see your Heavenly Father as one who presents idle bluffs? Maybe you were a victim of idle threats of a punishment that was never carried out.
- Do YOU see the Lord with no mercy or compassion? Perhaps you feel like you never received compassion or mercy from others.
- Do YOU see a God whose forgiveness you don't truly feel you deserve? Perhaps you still carry guilt from the past for something you were unable to pay. Do you feel as though you are still paying for your wrongs?

Others see the Lord God through you and your lifestyle…

What fruit or body language do I feed those around me?
(Circle the examples that apply to you and write down others you come up with.)

Hope	Resentment	Bitterness	Trust	Faith
Co-dependency	People-pleasing	Stubbornness	Distrust	

_____
_____

Jeremiah 23:2—*"Ye have scattered my flock, and driven them away, and have not visited them."*
Do I know that someone is offended with me and yet I run a different direction? If so, why don't I check on them and restore what's broken?

_____
_____
_____

Let's look at the other side.
Have I been influenced by someone else's undealt-with wounds or opinions?
If so, how has it affected me?
- Maybe I formed opinions about others without knowing them or the truth for myself?
- Maybe I have seen someone who was hurt by another who stabbed them in the back, so now I distrust that person because of a perception gained through someone else's experience.

_____
_____
_____
_____

Was I offended and I ran? What situations do I need to address or who is the person I need to face, even if it's myself?

If I cannot face a given situation, where do I go for comfort or to self-medicate instead of going to the Lord?

- As an example of self-medication, Adam self-medicated to relieve his shame by making fig leaves to cover Eve and himself.
- How might I self-medicate or cover up?
- Could it be through anger, like Cain, blaming others for the injury I caused and feeling justified? Could it be through TV, music, food, addictions, work, hunting, or even shopping? What are the things I use to escape or numb myself from reality?

_____
_____
_____
_____

Vs. 5—THE LORD WILL RAISE *"A RIGHTEOUS BRANCH"* (referring to Himself, Jesus Christ)!

The Lord will raise someone in right standing with Him to shepherd His people.

What is stopping me from being a righteous branch the Lord can use?
Do I believe in myself? Do I feel others cannot believe in me?
Do I feel like I have to live righteously before I can be used by the Lord?

_____
_____
_____
_____

The thing that stops us is unbelief.
This is the opposite of faith, and faith without works is dead.
You don't have to be clean to come to the Lord God. Come to God through the Lord Jesus to be cleansed.

Jeremiah 33:4-22

In vs. 6-7, the LORD, the God of Israel, said, *"Behold, I will bring health and cure ... and will reveal to them the abundance of peace and truth. I [God] will cause the captivity of Israel to return and will build them."*

Where do I need peace and truth revealed (whether it is the truth of others, the truth of a situation, or the truth within myself)? Wherever there is no peace or truth, I and everyone under me is a prisoner of war in a stronghold. What am I or someone under me held captive by? What area do I or others under me struggle with, still trying to find victory or freedom from?

_____
_____
_____
_____

Vs. 8—The LORD will cleanse us from the iniquity that caused us to sin against Him.

The iniquity is the root (emotions, if left undealt-with, will lead) to your actions. These may include self-rejection, self-protection, anger, jealousy, or control.

What thoughts or emotions do I have that cause me to heed another's voice, even a voice from within, and I follow that voice instead of the unction of the Holy Spirit, causing me to go against the LORD God?

_____
_____
_____
_____

Vs. 11-12—Being obedient to the LORD's voice causes us or others under us to return from the captivity of the land, and then there shall be a habitation of shepherds causing their flocks to lie down. We get peace and can share the LORD's peace with others, causing us to be a righteous branch instead of one that scatters.

In what areas can the LORD use me to bring peace, making me a peacemaker (see Matthew 5:9)?

_____
_____
_____
_____

— Notes —

Chapter 10

Spiritual Idolatry

I want you to honestly consider whose inheritance you are pulling from—THE LORD GOD'S OR SATAN'S?

There are two fathers in the Bible!

- _____
- _____

John 8:31-47
Vs. 31-43—Abraham's seed from Father God
Vs. 42—(_____)

Vs. 44-47—The devil's children: *"your father the devil"*
Vs. 44—(_____)

_____ Inner vows, acting on judgment

_____ Discernment

_____. Struggles with thorns and thistles

_____ Your inheritance

_____ Tragedy, loss, trauma

- According to which father we are loyal to, we will see the fruit of it manifesting in our lives.
- This is a way of seeing where our trust and loyalty lie.

This helps you to determine where your loyalty is deep within you.
Is it where you say it is?
- I know there are exceptions to this. You may be a caretaker, have children or work and you have to attend to your responsibilities. The Word of God separates and discerns the thoughts and the intent of the heart (Hebrews 4:12).

Do your words and actions line up? IF NOT, COULD THIS be a sign of idolatry within?
- What voices do we heed before God's?

Hebrews 9-12 (READ ALL THREE CHAPTERS ON YOUR OWN)

Hebrews 9:11-14
- 9:11 speaks of the blood atonement for sin. Adam covered himself with fig leaves, but the Lord God covered him with animal skins (the shed blood covered and atoned for the sin).
- In Genesis 9:5-6, with Noah, God said that He requires the blood of our lives at the hand of man or at the hand of every man's brother.
- 9:14—The blood of Christ purges our **conscience** from dead works.

What are the dead works in our lives and why would the Lord God have to purge us from them?

_____
_____
_____

Hebrews 12:1-6
- When Christ was in the garden praying to His Heavenly Father, He got to the point of sweating great drops of blood. Extreme stress can physically cause a body to do this.
- COULD it be that we get to a place where we are faced with anxiety and fear and we actually worship and obey that over God, while using that very same anxiety and fear as a justification, or excuse, to cover our actions?
- Hebrews 12:3-4—We must *"resist unto blood, striving against sin."* What are we resisting to the point of blood?
- COULD it be the voices screaming at us, voices of betrayal, rejection, abandonment, hurts, lies, perceptions, conscience, etc.?

Hebrews 12:7-13
Vs. 7—IF you are to be a son, you have to allow chastisement, the Lord God's discipline. Chastisement allows our Heavenly Father (God) to sit on the throne of your heart and not you.

Vs. 8—Without chastisement, you are a partaker and not a true son.

What exactly is the chastisement we go through to become a son?

_____
_____
_____

Can you take corrective criticism, or do you find yourself getting defensive or easily offended?

_____
_____
_____

When you are low on finances, and the Lord God says, "Trust Me," do you:
- a. Trust Him in all areas but the one area you struggle trusting Him in, resulting in the partaking of the tree of knowledge?
- b. Serve out your own wisdom again and do what "you think" best?
- c. Still rely on God?
- d. Merge yourself and God on the throne of your heart at the same time?
- e. Recognize where your trust and sincere loyalty lies?

1 John 4:1-6 speaks of testing every spirit and our discernment. We must know what we are looking for.

NOW, let's look at the two fathers:

<u>GOD VS. SATAN</u>	<u>PART OF THE TREE</u>
1 John 4:7-21 (focus on vs. 7-8) **GOD** • God is love (see 1 Corinthians 13). • Everyone who loves is born of God. • If you do not love, you don't know God. **SATAN** • Has torment (vs. 18) • There is no fear in love. • *Perfect [mature] love casteth out fear.*	_____—Where we are truly grounded. This is where we find out where our loyalty and trust truly rests. GOD—_____ SATAN—_____
GOD **1 Corinthians 13:1-10** • The definition of what love is • Love is a choice, who you are. • It's NOT a feeling. • *Rejoice not in iniquity, but in truth.* (Iniquity must be the lie)…	_____—Our support, strength. This is where our thought process is. This is where you make your thoughts obedient to Christ. This is where you choose to love your brother and not judge or be envious. ***This grows from the root.***

SATAN

Romans 1:25

"Who changed the truth of God into a lie, and worshipped ... the creature more than the creator."

This is where it all began. Adam started with complete trust and loyalty, then believed a lie and partook (trespass) of the tree of knowledge, allowing _____ _____ to enter.

Romans 7:9

"For I was alive without the law once: but when the <u>commandment</u> came, sin revived, and I died."

The commandment is my precept, law, (mindset)
- I'm saved and put under grace. Then something happens, causing me to have a choice to see if I trust God as my Provider or if I will put myself on the throne of my heart again.
- I serve and protect the lie (mindset, survival mode) that I operate through.
   <u>Example</u>: If I believe I'm rejected, then I will self-reject before giving others the opportunity to reject me.

Isaiah 14:12-15 (Lucifer said in his heart)
- <u>I will</u> ascend into heaven.
- <u>I will</u> exalt my throne above ...
- <u>I will</u> sit also upon the mount.
- <u>I will</u> ascend above the heights.
- <u>I will</u> be like the Most High.

GOD—_____ _____.

SATAN—_____
   (covers your iniquity)

He deceives us into being *our own god,* and we then build _____ to protect the lie we choose to continue to believe.

What does pride cover?
_____
_____
_____

How does pride cover?
_____
_____
_____
_____

GOD

Exodus 20:1-17 and Deuteronomy 5:7-21
- The 10 Commandments
- They are to be a guard, judge, or divide our actions.
- Galatians 3— The Law was our tutor.
- It sets a boundary or guardrail for my life.

SATAN

Proverbs 6:16-19
- Lists the six things God hates.
- The seventh is an abomination to God.

_____—reach out to the sun for nourishment.

GOD—Are we letting the Holy Spirit _____ us and refusing to remain offended?

SATAN—Are we _____ ourselves allowing offense to form, leading us to self-protect (one example)?

GOD

Galatians 5:22-26
- The nine fruits of the Spirit
- Vs. 23—Where fruits are, no law in them—freedom

SATAN

Galatians 5:16-21
- Fruits from working in the flesh
- If you manifest these fruits, you will not inherit the Kingdom, and you will not enter the garden!

_____—What people see, healing power or poison (your reality, testimony, and your freedom or bondage).

GOD—Our lifestyle (reality) will show if our loyalty and trust is _____ _____. People will see peace, assurance, and the hand of God.

SATAN—Our lifestyle (reality) will show us or others _____, stress, anxiety, uncertainty, maybe an unrealistic God or one who will let you suffer for no reason.

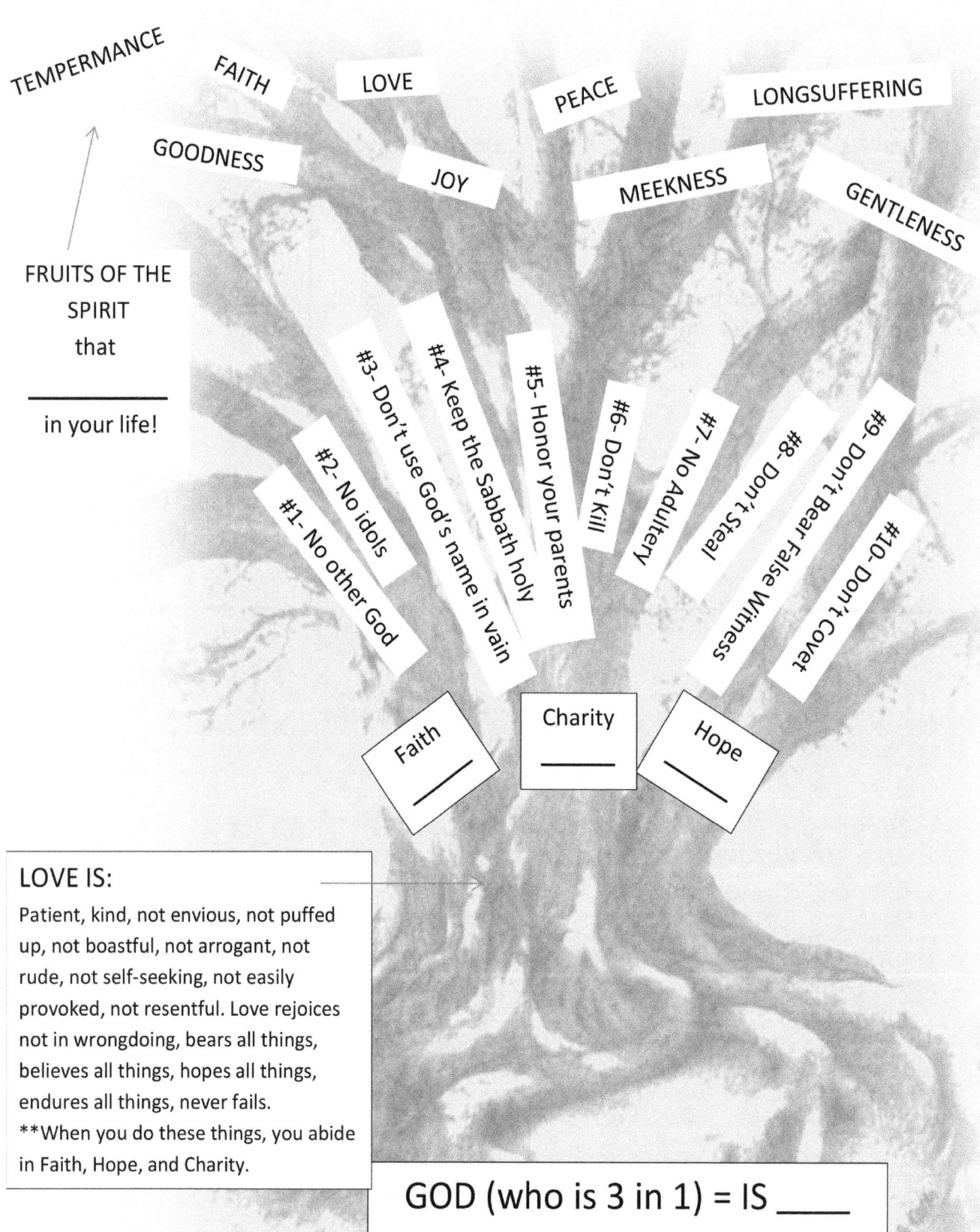

TREE OF LIFE

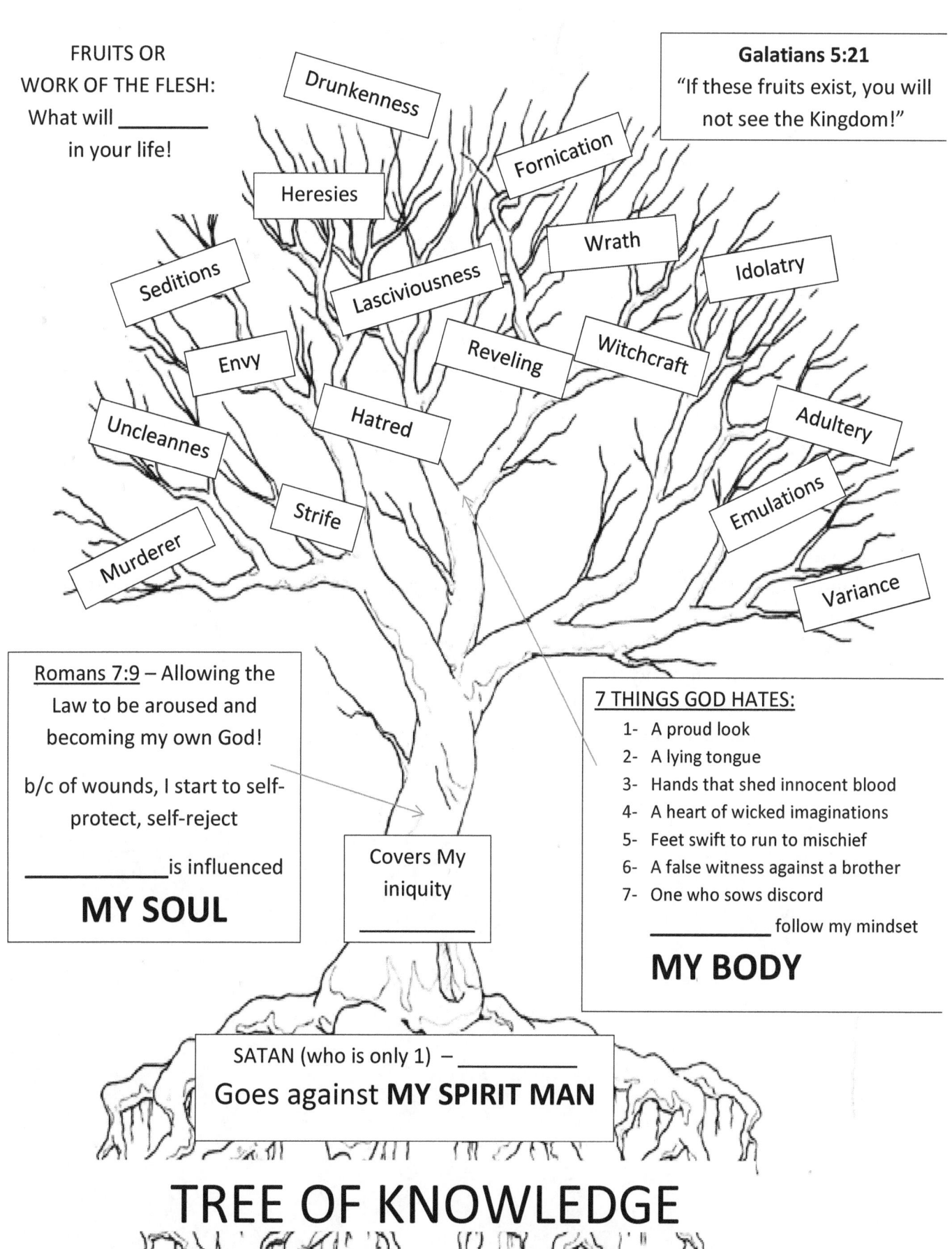

God is your Father IF_____ _____ _____ _____, you pull
from the Tree of LIFE!.

Satan is your father IF _____ _____ _____ _____, you pull
from the tree of the knowledge of good and evil!

1 John 3:10-12
  We see that Cain pulled in the inheritance of _____, _____ _____ ____ _____ _____.

Homework:
- Continue to record breakthroughs and revelations as you receive them in your quiet time with the Father.
- Check and comment on the Blog (if one was created).
- Continue journaling daily from His Word.
- Complete the questionnaire that follows.
- Using your answers from the questionnaire, complete the Idolatry Tree.

QUESTIONNAIRE:

In what area or areas do I play god by taking matters into my own hands, feeling justified in my actions, partaking of the tree of knowledge?

_____
_____
_____
_____
_____
_____

Think of God's names (Psalm 23):

Jehovah-Jireh (Genesis 22:14)—**The Lord is my Provider.**
- What is something I am trusting the Lord for? This can be financially (a job)? It could be an opportunity (the Lord opens the door for me).
- Or do I provide for myself and my family?
- Do I provide protection (even maybe over my children), causing trouble between myself and my spouse?

_____
_____
_____
_____
_____
_____

Jehovah-Rophi (Exodus 15:26)—**The Lord is my Health, Healing Physician.**
- Do I lean on my knowledge or on a doctor's ability, turning to the Lord when a sickness is incurable?
- Do I blame others if I get sick, casting judgment? (Example: They knew their kids were sick, and they came anyway.)

_____
_____
_____
_____
_____
_____

Jehovah-Nissi (Exodus 17:15)—**The Lord is my Flag, Banner, Victory.**
- Do I have to be the one to make sure my name remains clear, and no one has a bad image of me?
- Does the Lord get the glory (credit) for maintaining my good name or my success, or do I?

_____
_____
_____
_____
_____
_____

Jehovah-M'kaddesh (Exodus 31:13)—**The Lord is my Holiness, Sanctification.**
- *Sanctification* means "to make holy, set apart, to purify or free from sin."
- This also relates to the Sabbath, setting oneself apart and having time with the Lord.
- Or do I only feel clean if I deserve it? If I have suffered enough, but not because of the cross?
- Do I feel, in my situation, as though the Lord may be punishing me?

_____
_____
_____
_____
_____
_____

Jehovah-Shalom (Judges 6:24)—**The Lord is my Peace.**
- Peace is the opposite of strife. Or do I comfort myself (self-medicating) with food, a movie and/or shopping?
- Do I have peace only once I know the ending or if things are happening according to my plan?
- Do others see the Lord through my peace, or do they see me manipulating and controlling things to maintain my peace?

_____
_____
_____
_____
_____
_____

Jehovah-Rohi (Psalm 23:1)—**The Lord is my Shepherd**.
- Or do I lead myself?
- Do I make a plan or decision and then ask the Lord to bless it rather than asking Him first what plan or decision I should make?
- Do I allow the Holy Spirit to lead and direct my life, or do I make my own plans?
- Have I considered why my Heavenly Father may be leading me into temptations? Maybe for true repentance (Matthew 6:13)?

_____
_____
_____
_____
_____
_____

Jehovah-Tsidkenu (Jeremiah 23:6)—**The Lord is my Righteousness**.
- *Righteousness* means "quality or state of being righteous."
- Do I do things by my own ability and strength and what I feel is right, causing me to be the judge again, sitting on the throne of my heart?
- Is my righteousness based on my child's performance?
- Is my righteousness based on other relationships?

_____
_____
_____
_____
_____
_____

Jehovah-Shammah (Ezekiel 48:35)—**The Lord is there, omnipresent**.
- Do I feel as though the Lord is not always there and doesn't do what His Word says, so I take matters into my own hands?
- Do I see the Lord as someone who can always relate to how I feel?
- Do I even truly open my heart to reconstruct my opinion of the Lord?

_____
_____
_____
_____
_____

Cain had a choice to pull from either father. What was his choice?
- He chose to hide the iniquity (the undealt-with perception) when challenged to do what was right rather than dealing with the suppressed emotions when the Lord was confronting the issue at hand.
- He chose to pull from his father, the devil.
- (Second generation seen) Cain now murdered Abel in the physical through offense toward the Lord and suppressed emotions of rejection.
- Ultimately this caused Cain to walk away from the Lord's manifest presence.

What is the Lord wanting me to confront and expose? (BE HONEST)
_____
_____
_____
_____
_____
_____
_____

What will happen when I confront or expose it?
_____
_____
_____
_____
_____
_____

What have I been secretly battling? If not myself, what do I see my family and loved ones battling with:
- Lust?   ° Jealousy?   ° Lying?   ° Being judgmental?
- Failure?   ° Never being good enough?   ° Distrust?   ° Anxiety?
- Envy?   ° Anger?   ° Self-hatred?   ° Self-rejection?   ° Depression?

_____
_____
_____
_____

SPIRITUAL IDOLATRY

Tree of Knowledge –
    I'll do things **MY** way!

Tree of Life –
    I'll do things **GOD'S** way!

— Notes —

Chapter 11

Introduction to the "Destroy" Door

FORNICATOR:
- "A prostitute; to sell into slavery (today it looks like victim mentality)."
- Metaphorically: one bribed to give himself up wholly to another's will. To dispose of as merchandise or into slavery.

Do we spiritually prostitute ourselves to our idols (becoming a rival with God) and become a slave to our own emotions? (Example: a rival to peace could be anxiety.)

_____
_____
_____
_____

PROFANER:
- "Accessible, lawful to be trodden, unhallowed, common, public place."
- *Webster's*: "to treat something sacred with irreverence or disrespect."

How do we show disrespect to God's house? To God's Word? To the Holy Spirit? To our own vessel? To those in authority over us?

_____
_____
_____
_____

BLASPHEMY:
- *Webster's*: "Not showing respect or reverence in utterance or action concerning God or sacred things. The crime of assuming to ONESELF the rights or qualities of God (taking something lightly)."

Do we do this?
How do you feel when you have put a lot of time into something and it is trampled or overlooked?
Have you taken something for granted or shown disrespect and expected it to be overlooked, without thinking of how it would affect the other person?

_____
_____
_____
_____

BIRTHRIGHT:
- The birthright or advantage of the first born son, a privilege.
- *Webster's*: "A particular right of possession or privilege one has from birth, especially as eldest child."

Do we take our responsibilities (spiritually) lightly, thinking they will only affect us and not others?
Do we let our guard down or sell our authority for the temporary pleasure of maintaining an image or for a mere emotion?

_____
_____
_____
_____

We know Satan is looked at as Pride, which pride covers a _____ ___ _____.
What is pride?

_____
_____
_____
_____

Read Ezekiel 28:12-19 to see how Satan works:
- Vs. 12—*"Sealed up the sum," "full of wisdom,"* and *"perfect in beauty."*
- Look at the two things Satan offered Adam and Eve and still offers us today.
  ◦ *"Full of wisdom"*—He offered for them to be wise in their own eyes.
  ◦ *"Perfect in beauty"*—He offered vanity, pride (to cover ourselves).
- Vs. 13—*"Thou hast been in Eden the garden of God; every precious stone was thy covering,"* (referring to Lucifer).
- Pride doesn't want you to look or feel weak; pride provokes us to keep an image (it's all about self-image).
- The Scriptures say, *"forsake not the assembling of yourselves"* and *"confess your faults one to another."*

Sometimes through talking with others about offenses we carry, the truth can be revealed. What are the faults (a lapse or deviation from the truth, offense) we are to confess?

_____
_____
_____
_____

Why would guarding against pride or false humility be so important?

_____
_____
_____
_____

- Vs. 14—*"The anointed cherub that covereth"*
- Vs. 15—He was perfect *"TILL INIQUITY WAS FOUND in thee."* This means Lucifer also had free will.
- Vs. 16—Tells us the iniquity: *"By the multitude of thy merchandise they have filled the midst of thee with violence, and thou hast sinned: therefore, I will cast thee as PROFANE ... ."*
   ° He was called a profaner because of the multitude of merchandise!
   Merchandise means "to traffic or trade." Satan's merchandise started with music.

What do we trade and receive in return?

_____
_____
_____
_____

- Vs. 17—*"Corrupted thy wisdom by reason of thy brightness"*
- Vs. 18—*"Defiled thy sanctuaries by the multitude of thine iniquities, by the iniquity of thy traffick."*

John 2:12-25 (words of Jesus)
- Vs. 16—*"Make not my Father's house an house of merchandise."*
- Vs. 19—*"Destroy this temple, and in three days I will raise it up!"*
- Vs. 21—He was speaking of the temple of His body!

What within us do we trade with Satan and how?

_____
_____
_____

Maintaining Generational Freedom | 148

Genesis 25:29-34
- For a morsel of food, Esau sold his birthright.
- He "traded" his birthright with Satan for a payment.

What lie did Esau believe that allowed Satan to "merchandise" (manipulate or deceive) him?
_____
_____
_____
_____

What did Esau receive through this trade?
_____

What do you think are key notes in Esau's story that we can learn from to see how or why we might also sell our birthright and what we may receive in its place?

Vs. 29—_____
_____

Vs. 32—_____
_____

Vs. 33—_____
_____

Vs. 34—_____
_____

What is *"a morsel of food"* according to Hebrews 12?
_____
_____
_____
_____

What sustains us?   Example: Water sustains a fish. It can't live out of water. We were designed to be sustained by God, but do we trade God for comfort food, such as people's validations, instead of seeking God to validate and sustain us?
_____
_____
_____
_____

What lies does Satan get us to believe, saying words or making vows that lead us to break our covenants with the Lord, preventing us from being sustained in God?

_____
_____
_____
_____

What (in reality) do we trade our power, dominion or inheritance for today?

_____
_____
_____
_____

Esau _____ his birthright for a bowl of soup!

What trauma happened, or what did we hear growing up that we believe about ourselves that can cause us to sell or trade our inheritance?

_____
_____
_____
_____

Whichever part of God we don't know in our heart as His _____ _____, we are trading it off to _____ _____ to be that for us!

Homework
- Continue to record breakthroughs and revelations as you receive them in your quiet time with the Father.
- Check the Blog and comment (if one was created).
- Continue journaling daily from His Word.
- Complete the study on the God name Jehovah-Shammah, The Lord Omnipresent.

JEHOVAH-SHAMMAH

Psalm 23:4 *"Yea, though I walk through the valley of the shadow of death, I will fear no evil: for thou art with me; thy rod and thy staff they comfort me."*
The LORD is there, omnipresent (Ezekiel 48:35, the name of the city).

Psalm 139:1-10
 The LORD is searching my heart when I sleep and when I wake, my thoughts and what's on my tongue.
 Vs. 5—The LORD was surrounding him.
 Vs. 8—Whether I'm in Heaven or Hell, You are there.

What area of my life feels like I am experiencing Heaven, meaning there is peace?
_____
_____
_____
_____

What area of my life do I struggle with, as if I were experiencing Hell (where I feel I am tormented and can't seem to do what I want to do)?
_____
_____
_____
_____

How could I benefit by allowing the LORD to search my heart while I feel like I am experiencing Heaven (inner and outer peace) or Hell (inner or outer turmoil)?
_____
_____
_____
_____

Malachi 3:2-3—The LORD is the fire and soap! This is His purging process. If you allow the LORD to purge you, YOU, YOUR FAMILY, MINISTRY, AND OTHERS AROUND YOU WILL REAP THE BENEFITS OF IT!

Psalm 107:10-22

According to verses 10 and 11, why do we sit in darkness (with no answers) and in the shadow of death?

_____
_____
_____
_____

According to verses 12 and 13, the Lord brought their heart down with labor (trouble), and there was NO ONE around to help. What could the Lord be trying to break me from?

_____
_____
_____
_____

According to verse 14, the Lord brings you out of darkness and the shadow of death and breaks the bands in sunder.

Breaks means "to root out."

Bands means "the bonds or ties that make me a prisoner." (Example: self-protecting or self-providing, vows, oaths, broken covenants, etc.).

The only way to stay in true freedom is for the Lord to ROOT OUT THE TIE (CHAINS) THAT BRING ME BACK TO PRISONER.

What are the chains, hurts, or offenses (a twisted or wrong way of perceiving things) the Lord needs to uproot in me?

_____
_____
_____
_____

- Vs.17—Because of their transgressions and iniquities they were afflicted.
- Vs. 18—Their soul abhorred ALL MANNERS OF MEAT, and they drew near to gates of death.
- Vs. 19—"*THEN they cry unto the Lord, ... and he saved them out of their distresses.*"

To have a shadow, there has to be light.

A shadow is always bigger than the object it represents and looks like something it is not! This can feel intimidating (think about shadow puppets.)

The Lord is in the valley with you!

Our perception (offenses) and fear can make a thing seem bigger than it is and harder to overcome! The Scriptures say, *"confess"* and *"be healed"* (James 5:16-20).

What shadow, lie, or fear that lies dormant in my conscience is the Holy Spirit's light showing me in myself? What is the fear I have to look in the eye and confront? (Examples: Fear of rejection, fear of obligation, fear of a false responsibility, fear I am not being heard, etc.)

_____
_____
_____
_____

Psalm 139:11-24

Vs. 23-24—*"Search me, O God, and know my heart: try me, and know my thoughts: and see if there be any wicked way in me, and lead me in the way everlasting."*

"Search me and know my heart, try me and know my thoughts." Do I ask God to search me and try me, to test me so I can see and know my own thoughts? Or do I avoid my part (my responsibility) and try to cast blame on others, even the devil?

_____
_____
_____
_____

The deepest darkness isn't too dark for the Lord God. Even before I was born, while I was still in the womb, He saw me. He is omnipresent. I cannot escape Him!
Looking back to the times I went through the darkness and the valley, it proves to me and my emotions that the Lord God was always there and always will be!

Looking back now, where do I see the Lord God's goodness, His hand, and guidance at work in my life—even if I didn't recognize it back then?

_____
_____
_____
_____

Chapter 12

Four Judgments in Ezekiel

What are possible offenses that we could be purged from?

_____
_____
_____

Numbers 11:1-6 (refer to James 1:12-15)
- Complaining displeases the LORD.
- They fell lusting (intense craving) and asking for flesh to eat because they remembered Egypt.

When the Israelites allowed thoughts and memories of Egypt to be aroused, it caused their hearts to emotionally turn back to Egypt (as mentioned in Acts).

Think about what we could inherit from our forefathers (iniquities that resulted in them going back into the wilderness) that we need to renounce.

_____
_____
_____

Revelation 22:14
> "Blessed are they that do his commandments, that they may have right to the tree of life, and may enter in through the gates into the city."

Exodus 20:2-6—This was the beginning of a covenant.
- Vs. 1—The LORD their God spoke the commandments. They were given verbally to Moses and the people.
- Vs. 2—The LORD thy God brought us out of the land of Egypt, out from a house of bondage (slave or servant). This is spiritual freedom (not salvation)!

153

- He then gave us the 10 Commandments to stop us from going back into Egypt, which is our bondage!
  - These are the guardrails or guidelines that help keep us in check so that we may have the right to pull from the Tree of Life.
- Vs. 4-6— In Commandment #2, I have compared some key words from multiple translations:
  - A *graven image* (KJV), *image,* (NIV), *idol,* any form or manifestation (AMP)
  - *Visiting the iniquity of the father* (KJV)
  - *Punishing the children for the sin of their parents* (NIV)
  - *Visiting (avenging) the iniquity (perversity or guilt) of the fathers on the children (that is calling the children to account for the perversity or moral corruption of their fathers* (AMP).
  - Iniquity visits up to the third and fourth generation OF THEM THAT HATE ME.

Exodus 31:18—The Lord gave Moses the first set of written commandments.

Exodus 32—When the people grew tired of waiting on Moses, they made a golden calf to worship.

Exodus 34:1—The Lord said to Moses, "Come up with two more tablets, and I'll write on them like the first ones you broke," even though the Lord never told Moses to break them.

Think of times you may have had an easier victory or journey the first time, but the second time you had to work a lot harder for what you had so easily lost.

_____
_____
_____

Exodus 34:6-9

Vs. 7—**The Lord God** forgives **the iniquity, and the transgression, and the sin,** but, BY NO MEANS, CLEARS the guilty (leaving them unpunished); visiting (reckoning or avenging) the iniquity (sin or guilt) of the father upon the children and the children's children, unto the third and fourth generation.

What is iniquity?

___

What is transgression?

___

What is sin?

___

What is guilt?

___

The scriptures we read about the 10 Commandments say that the LORD God visits the iniquity of the fathers upon the children. Let's see why iniquity follows the family line.

Genesis 9:1-7
God blessed Noah when he got off the ark. What was the difference between Adam's blessing and Noah's blessing?

___

9:5—*Require* means "to demand an account of" (same word as in Ezekiel 14:3).

If someone does NOT deal with their emotions and doesn't face their situation, seeking the truth, the iniquity goes to the next person in the family line. If someone acts on their emotions and sheds innocent blood, it will NOT go unpunished. If they don't atone for it, it will continue until someone does atone for it.

We teach our children by what we do.

- Genesis shows that every seed reproduces after its kind.
- Genesis 34:25-31, generational iniquity. (Here they are vindicating themselves).
- Genesis 15:16—Travels until the iniquity is *"full."*

Matthew 27:11-25
- Jesus appeared before Pilate, and Barabbas was released instead.
- Vs. 24-25—The multitude declared, *"His blood be on us and on our children."*
- Here we see it spoken again—the punishment will travel to the children.

What idols, vows or oaths do you see or feel you or your family are living out where you see a pattern of it flowing through the place of your heart where the Lord God should reside?

_____

_____

_____

_____

Ezekiel 14
- This chapter is about a heart condition (idols of the heart), and turning to the Lord our God, and how the Lord _____ our attention.
- Read the chapter yourself and follow along with some of the key points below.

Vs. 3-5
- If you continue to put the idols in your heart _____ the Lord God, He will answer _____ to the multitude of your idols.
- You may think you hear the Lord, and you do, but the Lord may be allowing you to hear what you want to hear.

    (Refer to 1 Kings 22:22, where God sent a lying spirit.)

Vs. 7
- The process through which the Lord answers us

Vs. 8
- The LORD is the one who will cut you off from the midst of His people. Are there times that we blame Satan for something, and maybe it's not him at all?

The LORD's judgments are ALWAYS REDEMPTIVE in nature.

These are the four judgments the LORD will use to purge idols from your heart.

They are like the layers of an onion, each one getting closer to the heart!

The First Judgment

Ezekiel 14:13—"I [the LORD] ... will **BREAK** [wreck, crush, and destroy] the **STAFF** [tribe, rod, branch of vine] of the **BREAD** [the food, grain] thereof, and will **SEND** [let loose] **FAMINE** [hunger, figuratively God's Word] upon it, and will **CUT OFF** [eliminate] man and beast from it."

Vs. 14—If Noah, Daniel, and Job had been in this time period, they, too, could only have delivered themselves by their own righteousness.

What could be the food supply that feeds the walls to the idol or idols you listed above that the LORD could break, causing you to chase Him rather than HEEDING THE VOICE OF "THIS IS WITHIN MY ABILITY" (idol) so that you quit doing things on your own? (Your food supply is where you get your energy, nutrients, necessities, etc.)

_____
_____
_____
_____

Matthew 10:34-37
Why would the LORD send a sword to divide His people?

_____
_____
_____
_____

The Second Judgment

Ezekiel 14:15—*"If I [the Lord] cause **NOISOME BEASTS** [bad, evil, injury, calamity, misery] to **PASS THROUGH** [pass over, alienate, take away] the land, and they **SPOIL** [bereaved, make childless, miscarry – figuratively, fruit] it, so that it be **DESOLATE** [devastated, deserted, waste], that no man may **PASS THROUGH** because of the beasts."*

Vs. 16—If Noah, Daniel, and Job had been in this time period, they, too, could only have delivered themselves, BUT the land was to remain desolate.

1 Samuel 16:14—The Spirit of the Lord departed from Saul and a distressing spirit came. Why? Could Saul have possibly fought within, not passing the mantle over to David to be king?

What noisome beast could be passing through your life, causing you to lose your fruit? A noisome beast could be an intrusion, reality, or maybe even demons.

_____
_____
_____
_____

The Third Judgment

Ezekiel 14:17—*"If I [the Lord] **BRING** [to go in, enter, come, go, cause to come] **A SWORD UPON** that land, and say, Sword, **GO THROUGH** [pass over, alienate, take away] the land; so that I cut off man and beast from it."*

Vs. 18—If Noah, Daniel, and Job had been in this time period, they, too, could have only delivered themselves.

- ° *Sword* (could be our words or mouth)
- ° Maybe division, fighting or strife. These are external.
- ° Proverbs 13:2

Hebrews 12:4—*"Ye have not yet resisted unto blood, striving against sin."*

What would resisting *"unto blood"* look like when the Lord is bringing a sword through the land?

_____
_____
_____
_____

Do you act on your emotions?

_____
_____
_____
_____

Do you pay the debt (guilt) that's owed from your forefather, or do you repeat it?

_____
_____
_____
_____

NOTICE, the first three are _____; the fourth one is _____.

The Fourth Judgment

Ezekiel 14:19—*"If I [the Lord] **SEND** [let go, stretch out] a **PESTILENCE** [plague, disease] **INTO** that land, and pour out my **FURY** [heat, indignation, anger, wrath] upon it in blood, to cut off from it man and beast ..."*

Vs. 20—If Noah, Daniel, and Job had been in this time period, they, too, could only have delivered themselves by their righteousness.

° *"In the land"* means "in us!" A pestilence COULD BE sickness or disease.

What could the Lord be allowing to touch your spouse, your children, or even you yourself, to get your attention and get you to deal with heart issues (your conscience)?

_____
_____
_____

RECAPPING THE JUDGMENTS:

The First Judgment goes with the first door—**STEAL**.
- This is a separation so you can see what's happening.
- The Lord will break what feeds you if it's not Him. It is up to us if we are loyal and trust in Him or not.
- The Lord will have to separate you from a form of co-dependency (maybe the sword exists in your family and not peace) so you can see Him.
- Adam heeded another voice, an influence other than the voice of the Lord God.

What needs to **be broken** for the Lord to show you whose voice you are heeding?

_____
_____
_____
_____
_____
_____
_____
_____
_____

The Second Judgment goes with the second door—**KILL**.
- This is when you start to see the pattern.
- Cain acted outwardly because of emotions he was feeling inwardly. He felt alienated. The Lord wants to show you how to recognize what **is passing through** that prevents you from having good fruit.

What does your reality scream?

_____
_____
_____
_____
_____
_____

The Third Judgment goes with the third door—**DESTROY**.
- Are you starting to see that you have a part in the pattern?
- This is the sword, our mouth, what we say or tolerate what's being said!
- This is the beginning of the LORD starting to purge us now that He has our attention.

This is where we _____ _____ bloodshed, which is the ultimate pressure, not to sin, but to choose where we lay our trust and loyalty, removing ourselves and our family from under the curse we or others have placed us under.

What is it you are having to go against, not to repeat? What learned behavior, way of doing things, habit, or personality do you have to go against?
_____
_____
_____
_____
_____

The Fourth Judgment is to show us what is manifesting in our land, OUR HEART.
The LORD is showing us where we have _____ _____!

Homework:
- Continue recording any breakthroughs and revelations as you receive them in your quiet time with the Father.
- Check the Blog (if one was created).
- Continue journaling daily from His Word.
- Meditate on and answer the summary questions at the end of this lesson under the heading "Recapping the Judgments" honestly!
- Complete the trees and the questionnaire from Chapter 11 if you haven't finished them yet.

— Notes —

Chapter 13

NOAH AND THREE GENERATIONS

Are you a peacekeeper or a peacemaker?

_____
_____
_____
_____
_____

Noah cursed Ham's son Canaan because he exposed his *"nakedness"* (see Genesis 9:20-25). What was the nakedness that was exposed?

_____
_____
_____
_____
_____

Think about a time when something in your life or your children's life was exposed and brought shame, deceit or embarrassment. How did you respond? Did you try to cover it up? If so, how? What emotions arose within you? What if such a thing is exposed correctly and brought into the light in love?

_____
_____
_____
_____
_____

Maintaining Generational Freedom | 164

What if it is exposed incorrectly and NOT done out of love?

_____
_____
_____
_____

Isaiah 53:1-9
What does *"wounded for our transgressions"* mean?

_____
_____
_____
_____

What does *"bruised for our iniquities"* mean?

_____
_____
_____
_____

What does *"the chastisement of our peace"* mean?

_____
_____
_____
_____

Notice: *"By his stripes we ARE healed."* The three things above bring our healing.

- Vs. 6—*"Sheep ... gone astray"*
  - *"Turned every one to his own way"* (this is a _____ , when you turn).
  - Christ took everything on Himself (*"the iniquity of us all"*).
  - By taking our sin upon Himself, He redeemed us back to God, which is _____. (The annual blood sacrifice was no longer needed.)
  - He took the control back from Satan, giving us back our free will.

Vs. 7—"AND HE _____ _____ HIS MOUTH."
- Notice: this is the opposite of a fleshly reaction!

Why do you think it's important to keep quiet when you feel the iniquity rising? Remember, the iniquity is the root belief system (conscience) that leads to the feelings (consciousness) of why you do things (rejection, abandonment, etc.).

_____
_____
_____
_____

Read James 3:1-18

Vs. 2—We are all given the opportunity of an _____ to come and to _____.

Vs. 3—What controls you? You have the chance to be soul-led or Spirit-led.

Vs.6—"*The tongue is ... a world of iniquity.*" Think about Esau. He sold his birthright for a morsel of food with his _____.

Vs. 10—"*Out of the same mouth proceedeth* _____ *and* _____."

Vs. 11-12—The rivers are to come _____ us and _____ us to the world.

Vs.13—"*Godly wisdom*" means that person has "*a good conversation.*"

Vs.14-15—Earthly or devilish wisdom means that person speaks with bitter envying and strife FROM their _____.

Vs. 18—"*And the fruit of righteousness is SOWN IN PEACE of them that* _____ _____."

Luke 6:45

"*Of the abundance of the heart, the* _____ _____."

We can speak either good or evil.

Proverbs 17:1-3

    Vs. 1—*"Better is a dry morsel and quietness ..."*
       (This is the opposite of _____.)
    "Than an house full of sacrifices with strife."
       (This sounds similar to _____.)
       (Image or life of the church with _____, suppressed intimidation, jealousy, or envy)
    Vs. 2—*"A wise servant shall rule over a son that causeth shame."*
       (This makes you think of _____ (_____ _____).
    Vs. 3—*"The L*ORD* _____ the hearts!"*
       (We will go through a series of tests in life for the purpose of God showing us what is in our hearts.)

Proverbs 17:9

    "He that covereth a transgression seeketh love;
    but he that repeateth a matter separateth very friends."

- Repeating a matter refers to "_____."
- This is not maturity. This opens a door with "_____."
- If you want to remain free, WORK TO _____ ___ _____.

James 5:19-20

Proverbs 16:1-7

    Vs. 2—We are *"clean in _____ _____ ____, but the L*ORD* weighs the spirits."*
    Vs. 3—Turn back our works to the L*ORD* (the _____ is turning away).
    Vs. 5—None will go unpunished.
    Vs. 6-7—*"BY MERCY AND TRUTH INIQUITY IS _____:*
        AND BY THE FEAR OF THE LORD MEN _____ FROM EVIL."

- When your life is pleasing to God (because you allow chastisement), your enemies are made to be at peace with you.

Ezekiel 18:5-32

THE FIRST GENERATION

Verses 5-9 talks about a man:

- Who lives a _____ _____ .
- Who is _____ .
- Who _____ the Lord's commandments.
- This is equivalent to being _____ _____.
- This man shall "_____."

THE SECOND GENERATION

Verses 10-13—Talk about:

- The _____ of the just man from the first generation we just talked about.
- The son does _____ of the dad (the just man).
- This is equivalent to being _____-_____ (if it's the opposite of what the dad did.)
- Being soul-led is doing what is right in our own eyes _____ to how you see it.
- He disobeyed the Lord by being a _____ _____ _____ of blood.
- Notice that his disobedience CAUSED HIM TO _____ .
- Notice that his _____ shall be upon him.

THE THIRD GENERATION

Verses 14-17— Talk about:

- A son that is born from the _____ man.
- This son _____ everything his dad did, referring to the "_____ _____."
- Once he considered his father's lifestyle, he did _____ !
- Notice that the scripture says, "he SHALL NOT DIE FOR THE _____ _____ _____."
- The scripture says, "This man _____ _____."

BREAKING FREE: (vs. 19-32)

- Vs.19-21—We ___ ___ ___ we do what is right in the LORD's eyes!
- Vs. 26-28—We have ___ because we ___ and ___ ___.
- Vs. 30-31—True repentance is going in the opposite direction. This is going ___ ___ ___!

  A new heart is new ___, new ___, a renewed compassion for others.
  Iniquity is found in the heart.
  A new understanding is being willing to look past reality.
  A new spirit is a new ___.
  You can be soul-led and think you are following the LORD God, only to discover you are following ___.
  You can be Spirit-led and follow ___.

We are all born with a sinful nature, which is our soul and flesh.

We are told to "crucify" our flesh and follow the leading of the Holy Spirit.

Homework:
- Continue recording the breakthroughs and revelations you receive in your quiet time with the Father.
- Check and comment on the Blog (if one was created).
- Continue journaling daily from His Word.
- Complete the study on the God name Jehovah-M'Kaddesh, The LORD Is my Sanctification.

Jehovah–M'Kaddesh

Psalm 23:5 *"Thou annointest my head with oil; my cup runneth over."*
The Lord is Sanctification   (Exodus 31:13).

Read Exodus 31

31:1-11
- Vs. 3—*"And I have filled him with the Spirit of God, in wisdom, and in understanding, and in knowledge and in all manner of workmanship."*
- They were filled with the Spirit in the Old Testament to empower them to do what they were called to do.
- The materials for the Tabernacle and the workman to build it were carefully chosen.

31:13
- Keeping the Sabbath was a sign between the Lord and the people that they might know that He was the Lord who sanctified them!
- Notice that *sabbaths* here is plural.

31:14-17
- You can defile the Sabbath by doing any **work** on a day that is set apart.
- Vs. 14—*"Whosoever doeth any work therein, that soul shall be cut off from among his people."*
- **Not working** on the Sabbath was taken by the Pharisees from a legalistic point of view.
- The Scriptures say, *"Faith without works is dead."*

Biblically, the Sabbath is a time to cease, to rest, or a day of atonement. It's a time to stop, reassess, and reset.

What is the Sabbath to me?

_____
_____
_____

Read Mark 3:1-6 and paraphrase what I get from the story.

_____
_____
_____
_____
_____
_____

Maintaining Generational Freedom | 170

Read Luke 13:10-17 and paraphrase what I get from the story.

_____
_____
_____
_____

Read Matthew 12:1-14 and paraphrase what I get from the story.

_____
_____
_____
_____

According to what I've read, HOW can I defile the Sabbath today?

_____
_____
_____
_____
_____
_____
_____
_____

On many occasions, after Jesus had healed the sick and done many miracles, He would go aside alone to pray. Why would He do this?

Was He transferring the glory back to His Heavenly Father?

Think about what temptation could have taken place if Jesus had not stopped and transferred the glory back to the Father.

What do I transfer to my Heavenly Father when I give Him thanks?

_____
_____
_____
_____

Understanding a Sabbath will take you out of a religion and bring you into a relationship!
It's all about God, not us.
Pride makes it all about us, and pride covers shame, etc.
The Scriptures also say that God *"resisteth the proud"* (1 Peter 5:5).

Referring back to **Exodus 31,** let's look at how the Sabbath still benefits us today.
- Exodus 31:17 refers to it being a sign, a renewal, or of us being refreshed.

We are a three-part body with a three-part Trinity, so let's look at a sabbath in a three-part method. (Take time to write down anything else the Holy Spirit drops into your spirit about how you can relate the sabbath to your own personal life.)

A Physical Sabbath
- Your body needs a break, time to rest and rebuild itself, or you risk physical burnout.
- If your body stays in high gear (flight to flight, always on an adrenaline high), chemicals will be released into your body that you truly don't need, causing your physical body to break down.
-
-
-

A Mental Sabbath
- Your soul needs a break and time away as well. If you don't get breaks or time away, you could become emotionally overwhelmed and have a mental breakdown.
-
-
-

A Spiritual Sabbath
- Your spirit needs a time of rest, to keep you out of legalism or the "works" mode.
- This puts you in a relationship and out of a religion.
- This takes the burden off of us and gives it to Jesus.
- The Scriptures say, His *"burden is light."*
-
-
-

Which of these three aspects of the Sabbath do I need to practice applying more?

_____
_____
_____
_____

We are called to go from glory to glory (spiritually).

Physically, glory to glory looks like your convictions changing, bringing you to a deeper and more intimate walk with your Heavenly Father through our Lord Jesus Christ.

We are called to separate ourselves from all that is not holy!

What is God showing me that I need to start separating myself from?
Examples could be: friends, music, TV, or other things that have an influence over me.

_____
_____
_____
_____
_____
_____
_____
_____
_____
_____

Chapter 14

Malachi 1 and 2

What weight does a name carry?

_____
_____
_____

Reference: Mark 9:38-41—_____

_____
_____

Revelation 19:13

"And his name is called THE WORD OF GOD."

Malachi 1:1-5

I want you to put yourself in the setting of the book of Malachi and ask yourself:
- Do I feel that I am truly loved by the LORD?
- Have I ever truly felt loved by others?
- Have I ever truly felt the LORD's love?
- Do I feel the LORD's love only because the Bible says it?
- Do I ever look at what's happening around me and feel like I have done everything I could for someone else, to show them I love or support them, yet I end up feeling like they walked all over me, and I don't feel loved or respected?
- Do I find myself wondering at times if the LORD is punishing me because I never seem to get a break?

_____
_____
_____
_____
_____

173

Maintaining Generational Freedom | 174

Could this be what the Lord was expressing through His messenger Malachi? They were doing everything they knew to do for the Lord, and yet He saw their offering as polluted.

Vs. 4—*"Edom saith…"* Who was Edom?
Genesis 25:30—_____

Why was the Lord referring to the legacy Esau left behind, to not feel loved by the Lord, but, instead, feel hated?

Reference Genesis 25:21-28

What things happened that may have caused Esau to grow up and feel like his brother was loved by the Lord and others more than himself?

1. _____
_____
_____

2. _____
_____
_____

3. _____
_____
_____

Could the Lord be addressing a misguided mindset (iniquity, conscience) this rebellious generation has about Him?

Ask Yourself:
- Have I felt like others and even the Lord loves someone else more than me?
- No matter what I do, I can't seem to earn or feel their love, and yet the one (you perceive) they love can seem to do no wrong in their eyes?
- What repetitive saying was drilled into me?
- What has caused this mindset inside of me?

What mindset about the Lord do I have that He has to renew or even develop a whole new way of how I know Him (see Matthew 7:21-23)?

_____
_____
_____

Malachi 1:6-14

Vs. 6-7—"*A son honoureth his father, and a servant his master,*" and He is our Father. So, the Lord asks, "*Where's my honour? ... where is my fear? ... O priests that despise **MY NAME** ... offer polluted bread upon mine altar?*"

(*Honor* means two different things here.)

Vs. 8-14—Malachi tells us how we offer polluted bread and despise the Lord's name.

13—"*Thus you brought an offering: should I accept this of your hand? saith the Lord.*"

This is the same Hebrew word used with Cain and Abel.

14—Making a vow and not keeping it

What vows or covenants have I made that I have not kept?

_____
_____
_____
_____

What is honor?

_____
_____
_____
_____

Exodus 20:12—The first commandment that comes with a _____ attached.

"*Honour thy father and thy mother.*"

Honor, here in Exodus, refers to being "heavy, weighty, grievous, burdensome."

In Malachi, it is the same *honor* as in Exodus, when it refers to the honor a son gives to his father. But the Lord's honor is different. The Lord's honor means "glory, honor, glorious, abundance, reputation, or reverence."

<u>References on Honor:</u>

Mark 10:19—_____
_____

Maintaining Generational Freedom | 176

_____
_____
_____

Luke 18:20—_____
_____
_____
_____
_____
_____

Matthew 15:3-6—_____
_____
_____
_____
_____
_____

I should carry the _____!

For me to place my burden on someone else, even if it's the Lord, is _____!

Jesus willingly took our burden on Himself at the cross. Luke 9 tells us *"to take up [our] cross and follow [Him]."*

Where do I feel like I "HAVE TO DO" for the Lord (religion) instead of serving Him as an opportunity "I GET TO" attitude (relationship)? If I do all the right things (OUTWARDLY), but with a wrong attitude or motive, will the Lord ask me, "Should I accept this from your hands" (see Matthew 7:21-23)?

_____
_____
_____
_____

Ephesians 6:1-2
- Notice that it separates obedience and honor.
- *Obedience* means _____
  _____
- *Honor* means _____
  _____

According to Malachi, we despise the LORD's name.
- *Despise* refers to "holding in contempt (feeling that a person or thing is beneath consideration, worthless, or deserving scorn)."
- This same original word for *despise* is used in:

Genesis 25:34—

Numbers 15:31—

2 Samuel 12:9-10—

In what ways can I bring honor and return the glory to the LORD's name again (see Philippians 2:5-8)?

Matthew 15:18 (words of Jesus)
> "But those things which proceed out of the mouth come forth from the heart; and they defile the man."

Ironically, Matthew 15:3-9 speaks about honoring our father and mother, again referring to our traditions (which means our lifestyle or habits) taking the power out of the commandment by making it of none effect (see verse 6). Then we are called *hypocrites* because we draw near to God with our mouths, by saying the right things, honoring God with our lips, BUT our heart is far from Him.

So, if my speech defiles me, what are some ways I can cleanse my heart and stop polluting the Lord's table and His name?

_____
_____
_____
_____
_____

In what ways do I deceive myself by making a vow or covenant, saying things like, "I'll read more," "I'll pray more," "I'll take care of my parents," or agreeing to something that's said over the altar that I will do, then I don't do it and live with broken covenants and wonder why the Lord doesn't receive the offering from my hand?

_____
_____
_____
_____
_____

Reference: 1 Peter 2:9—We are a chosen generation, a royal _____, a holy nation.

Malachi 2
    Vs. 1-3—This commandment is for you!
    If you don't hear or don't lay it to heart to give glory to "_____ _____":
- I will **SEND A CURSE** upon you.
- **I WILL CURSE** your blessings.
- I will corrupt your seed (rebuking your descendants).
- I will spread dung upon your faces, even the dung of your solemn feasts.
- One shall take you away with it.

Reference: Job 32:1-2—_____
_____
_____

Do I apply the Word of God to my life?
Is God's living Word offensive to me?
In what area do I need to change my life to conform to the Lord God's Word instead of expecting His Word to conform to me?

_____
_____
_____
_____

    Vs. 5—*"My covenant was with him of life and peace; and I gave him for the fear wherewith he feared me, and was afraid before ____ _____."* (See Numbers 25:10-12).
- The covenant the Lord made with the Levites
- Deuteronomy 33:8-11 tells us what the Levites were responsible for.
- The Levites, at this time, didn't have a damaged mindset concerning the Lord.

Reference:
John 17:4, 6 and 11-12 (words of Jesus)

_____
_____
_____
_____

If it was so important for Jesus to bring honor and glory to the Father's name, how much more for me?

_____
_____
_____
_____

What fear did Levi have that we need to have too?
    Vs. 6
- *"The law of truth was in his mouth"* is referring to the Levite's speaking truth from _____ _____.
- *"Iniquity was not found in his lips"* is referring to the Levite's going through _____ _____. Both of these verses take place when we are a _____ because we believe a lie.

Maintaining Generational Freedom | 180

- ° *"He walked with me in peace and equity"* refers to the Levites' _____. This verse takes place when we are a _____ because this is the journey we walk through. We have to change the way we think and act.
- ° *"[He] did turn many away from iniquity"* refers to the Levites pulling others out of bondage, _____, teaching others to be Spirit-led and not controlled by emotions causes us to rise as a _____.

Where am I currently operating in the journey of verse 6? And what needs to be done to move me to the next part, so that I ultimately become a successful warrior?

_____
_____
_____
_____
_____
_____
_____

Vs. 7-9—*"Ye have corrupted the covenant of Levi"* by not keeping the Lord God's ways but being *"partial in the law."*

- Being *partial* refers to "lift, carry, take, to exalt oneself, to cause one to bear (iniquity)."
  <u>Reference</u>: 1 Samuel 2:12-3:14, when Eli had two sons who did wickedly, he knew about it and did nothing (see 2:22-24). Because Eli knew and turned his eyes away, the iniquity was judged and could not be purged by sacrifice or offering (see 3:13-14).

Hebrews 10:26 shows that there is *"no more sacrifice"* for **willful** sin after we have received the knowledge of the truth.

Where am I partial to the Lord God's Word, believing one part of it and not another?
Do I justify myself to others as to why I can do the Lord's will in this area and not in another, easing my guilt?

_____
_____
_____
_____
_____
_____

Where am I being affected or where have I been affected by partiality on the part of another person?

_____
_____
_____
_____
_____
_____

Vs.10-16—The Lord of Hosts went on to ask, *"Why do we deal treacherously every man against his brother?"* *"An abomination is committed."*

Here He addressed three types of offense or ways in which we deal treacherously:

Define *treacherously*:

_____
_____
_____

1. Against friends and his brother, profaning the covenant of the father (vs. 10)
2. Through spiritual idolatry
   ° Knowingly and continually doing something wrong and still bringing our offering to the Lord (vs. 11-12)
   ° He went on to describe dealing treacherously as marrying the daughter of a strange god.
   ° The Lord said that He will CUT OFF the man who does this from the Tabernacle.
3. Against the wife of your youth (vs. 13-14)
   ° The Lord went on to say that in order to stop dealing treacherously with the wife of your youth, you must take heed to the Spirit.

References:
Colossians 3:17-25—_____
_____
_____

Genesis 26:34-35 and 28:8—_____
_____
_____

Vs. 12—*"The Lord will cut off... the master and the scholar, out of the tabernacles of Jacob, and him that offereth an offering unto the Lord of hosts."*

    Master refers to "rousing oneself, awaken incite, or to awake."

    Scholar refers to "answering, responding, testify, speak, shout (to be aware of)."

Where have you been convicted and still deal treacherously or offensively with your Heavenly Father?

_____
_____
_____
_____
_____

In what areas has the Lord God told me to let go and let the Holy Spirit move in me, but I still keep my hands on the situation, enabling others, enabling myself to stay in self-pity, or enabling myself to maintain the perception I have of the Lord God because of the lessons retained from my injury, trauma, or offense?

_____
_____
_____
_____
_____
_____
_____

Do I justify myself, saying I can't change? Or am I honest with myself and ask for help?

_____
_____
_____
_____
_____
_____

Vs. 14—*"Because the Lord _____ _____ ___ _____ between thee and the wife of thy youth."*
- What is He a witness to?
  ◦ The vows, covenants or promises we have made.

- Remember Malachi 1:14, where it says, *"Cursed be the deceiver, which ... voweth"* and then breaks that vow!

Vs. 15-16—*"Take heed to your spirit, that ye deal not treacherously."*

What spirit do I heed?

_____
_____
_____
_____
_____

Vs. 17—You wearied the LORD with your words.
- We weary the LORD with our words because we don't mean what we say.
- When an opportunity presents itself to put action behind our words, we falter.

FAITH WITHOUT WORKS IS DEAD!

In what ways do I weary the LORD?

_____
_____
_____
_____
_____

References:
Hebrews 3:7-19
    Vs. 7—*"To day if ye will hear his voice ..."*
        ° Being Spirit-led is heeding the voice of the Spirit inside you.
        ° You can't enter His rest because of **unbelief**.

_____
_____
_____

Maintaining Generational Freedom | 184

Numbers 14:11-38

_____
_____
_____

After everything I have learned, the Lord is showing me that He is my Provider, Protector, etc. What is it that I refuse or struggle to believe, causing me to stay in unbelief?

_____
_____
_____
_____
_____
_____

Homework:
- Continue recording your breakthroughs and revelations as you receive them in your quiet time with the Father.
- Continue journaling daily from His Word.
- Check the Blog and comment when needed (if one was created).

Chapter 15

Malachi 3 and 4

Malachi 3

Vs. 1-2—A messenger was sent by the Lord to prepare a way.
- Suddenly, the Lord Himself showed up as a *"refiner's fire"* and *"fuller's soap."*

Vs. 3—The Lord comes to purify us by purging away the iniquity, BUT do we follow His leading? We all have free will. We have a choice to follow or rebel against the Lord.
- How? We have to start _____ what we learn and what the Holy Spirit shows us and convicts us of!

Vs. 4—Once we are purged and cleansed from the iniquity (the twisted mindset of how we see others, ourselves and the Lord), THEN the offering we bring will be pleasant and acceptable before the Lord.

Vs. 5—*"AND I will come near to you to judgment; and I will be a swift witness against"*:
- ***Sorcerers***, which refers to the practice of witchcraft (which is manipulation).
  References: Galatians 3:1, 1 Samuel 15:18-24 and Numbers 31:15-16
- ***Adulterers,*** which refers to both adultery and idolatrous worship.
  Reference: Exodus 22:20
- ***False swearers***, which refers to a lie, deception, to swear, take oath, or to curse.
  Reference: Exodus 23:1-9
- ***Those that oppress the hireling in his wages***, which refers to "a deceit, to extort the wages or pay."
- ***Those that oppress ... the widows***, which could refer to a spiritual widow as well as a physical widow. Spiritually, this is an area where there is a misconception in how we view the Lord God and Jesus as our Husband, Protector, and Provider (see Ruth 1:20-21).
- ***Those that oppress ... the fatherless***, which could refer to someone who is spiritually fatherless as well as physically fatherless. Spiritually, this is an area where there is a misconception in how we view the Lord God as the Father figure and the Holy Spirit, who is our Comforter, as the Mother figure.
  References for the widows and fatherless: James 1:26-27 and Exodus 22:22-24

Maintaining Generational Freedom | 186

- ***Those that ... turn aside the stranger***, which refers to "turning, to pervert, extend, influence the temporary inhabitant or the newcomer."
  <u>References</u>: Exodus 22:21 and Leviticus 22:17-33
- ***Those that ... fear not me***, which refers to "our reverence, to stand in awe, be afraid, honor, respect, a godly fear, or terrify."

Romans 1:18-25
- You _____ the truth that God showed you, for whatever reason, causing a cycle to start. This is the cycle of being turned over and putting you or your family back into spiritual prison.
- _____ can cause us to suppress the truth and continue circling the mountain. Unbelief and rebellion, according to Numbers 13 and 14, stopped the Israelites from going into the Promised Land. In Mark 9, we see a man asking the Lord to help his unbelief.
  ◦ In what area do I still have unbelief? Am I even asking the Lord to help me with my unbelief?

Which of the areas discussed in verse 5 need to be recognized, cleansed, and purified with fire and soap to make my offering pleasant and acceptable to the Lord?

_____
_____
_____
_____

<u>Reference Story:</u>
2 Samuel 12:9-16
    This was when the prophet Nathan confronted King David about killing Uriah and taking his wife, Bathsheba.

From this event, what possibly could have flowed in David's lineage after him?

_____
_____
_____
_____

2 Samuel 13:1-15
- This was when David's son _____ _____ and _____ his sister.
- Later on in the story, a brother killed this son because of what he had done.

- King David may have repented for the sin, but he didn't purge the _____ (which was the root of why all this happened) from his family line. Suppressing the iniquity, may have allowed it to remain _____ in his lineage, to manifest later in his children's lives, but it is also based on David's own judgment spoken out of anger, as the LORD was his witness. He reaped what he sowed, except that David would not die (see 2 Samuel 12:5-13).

What things do I know of that have been left dormant in my lineage?

_____
_____
_____
_____

Malachi 3:6—The LORD doesn't change; therefore, Jacob isn't consumed.
- The LORD remembers the promises and covenants He has made and doesn't consume us in our disobedience.
  Reference: Numbers 20-23

Vs. 7-12— Speaks of tithes **AND** offerings
- If we don't return tithes and offerings willingly and not grudgingly (which is entrusting and returning our heart fully to God), we are robbing God by breaking the covenant of the Levites and _____ ourselves under a curse!
- Tithing is a sign of the covenant.
- This is more than physically returning what is already God's.
- Remember, the chapters before talked about spiritual idolatry and dealing treacherously.

**We must have a right heart toward the LORD God and people
for Him to accept things from our hands.**

Vs. 7—*"Ye are gone away from mine ordinances. ... Return into me."*
Reference: Deuteronomy 30

Vs. 8—*"Ye have robbed me [God]."*
How have we robbed Him?

Maintaining Generational Freedom | 188

Read **Philippians 2:5-8,** which tells us how we can rob God today. Then, list them below:

_____
_____
_____
_____
_____

Vs. 9—You are cursed with a curse. Notice, we are _____ cursed!

Vs. 10—The tithes are for the Kingdom's sake.

Vs. 11—The Lord God rebukes the devour for our sake. He rebukes the devourer in two parts.
    1. He SHALL NOT destroy the fruits of our ground (plural).
    2. NEITHER SHALL our vine cast her fruit before its time.

Do I find myself in a situation in which the things I put my hands to do NOT prosper? Does discouragement and bitterness come before me as I am waiting on a promise to come to pass, perhaps because it hasn't happened in my timing yet?

_____
_____
_____
_____

References: 1 Timothy 6:10 and Matthew 6:24

Vs. 13—The Lord says that our words are *"stout"* against Him.
    How are our words *stout* against the Lord?

Vs. 14—*"Ye have said, It is vain to serve God, and what profit is it that we have kept his ordinance?"*

Reference: Leviticus 1-5 lists the various types of offerings:
Read them and then make your own notes to go with the various types of offerings we give:
- A Burnt Offering _____
_____

- A Grain Offering _____
- A Peace Offering _____
- A Sin Offering _____
- A Trespass Offering _____

Vs. 15-18

Vs. 15—Calls a proud person *"happy."*
This refers to those who work wickedness and tempt the Lord God.

Vs. 16—A Book of Remembrance is written for *"them that feared the Lord, **AND** that thought upon his name."*

Which of the above groups do I think I would fit into and why? Do I act properly, provoking others to come to the Lord God? Or do I provoke others to offense?

_____
_____
_____

Reference: Matthew 7:13-14

Vs. 17—*"I will spare them, as a man spareth his own son that _____ him."*

Vs. 18—*"THEN shall ye return and _____ again."*

Malachi 4

Vs. 1—*"The day cometh, that shall burn as an oven; and all the proud, yea, and all that do wickedly, shall be stubble."*

What is this stubble?

_____
_____

- 1 Corinthians 3:13-15—Talks about the fire.
    * It is in a fire that we see if _____ _____ burn away or stand.

Maintaining Generational Freedom | 190

- Luke 22:31-32—Jesus told Peter that Satan desired _____ into his (Peter's) life.
    * Satan asked God if he could sift Peter as wheat. He wanted permission to put Peter through a fire, a hard time, to try to pull him down.

- The scripture also states that the fire will leave no branch or root.

- Hebrews 12:11-17—Refers to the chastening of a father.
    * Because we endure the chastening and choose _____ ___ ___ _____, we produce the fruit of righteousness.
    * Our hands that hang low and our weak knees are no longer lame, but rather we have been healed.
    * Hebrews warns us NOT to allow a root of bitterness to spring up, referring to _____.
    * Think of the tree diagrams we have been working on. What branch (our belief) or root does the LORD God need to burn out of our heart (Romans 11:19-21)?

Vs. 2-3—"**<u>BUT UNTO YOU THAT FEAR MY NAME SHALL</u>** the Sun of righteousness arise with healing in his wings."

1. "Ye shall go forth, and grow up as calves of the stall."
    * You will _____ and grow.
2. "Ye shall tread down the wicked; for they shall be ashes under ... your feet."
    * This is _____ over the enemy.

Notice: Malachi closed the chapter with verse 6, basically letting us know that we have the choice of _____ or a _____. We can turn hearts to each other, which will bring _____, or away from each other through offense or prejudice, which will bring _____. The choice is ours. We bring a curse on ourselves when we honor anything (physical or emotional) or anyone before the LORD God (see 1 Samuel 2:29)!

<u>References:</u>
Exodus 20:3-6
Jeremiah 17:5

Look at Matthew 10:34-39 in two parts (words of Jesus):

Part 1:
> * Jesus came to bring a sword, not peace.
> * If you love your father and mother more than Me, you are not worthy of Me.
> * If you love your son or daughter more than Me, you are not worthy of Me.

Part 2:
> * He who takes **not** his cross and follows Me is not worthy of Me.
> * Carrying your cross refers to putting the Lord God's truths above your own perceived truths.

NO PARTIALITY!

<u>Reference</u>: 1 Samuel 15:1-24

_____
_____
_____
_____

Homework:
- Continue recording your breakthroughs and revelations as you receive them in your quiet time with the Father.
- Continue journaling daily from His Word.
- Check the Blog and comment when needed (if one was created).
- Complete the study on the God Name "Jehovah-Nissi," The Lord is my Banner and Flag.

JEHOVAH-NISSI

Psalm 23:5 *"Thou preparest a table before me in the presence of mine enemies."*
The LORD is my Banner or Flag (Exodus 17:15).

<u>Nissi</u> refers to "a flag, a standard, a signal, or a sign."

Highlights of Moses' story from Exodus 1-16:
- Moses was born a Hebrew and raised an Egyptian. He later killed an Egyptian and fled from Pharaoh.
- In chapter 3, The LORD spoke to him through a burning bush and told him to go back and set His people free. God is a covenant-keeping God (see Exodus 2:24-25).

Exodus 3:11-4:17
- Moses' first response to the LORD's call was his insecurities.
  - The First Insecurity—low self-worth (see 3:11)
    * Who am I? could refer to not feeling good enough or able to be used, a "why me?" feeling.
  - The Second insecurity—Not knowing what to say about who the LORD is (see 3:13).
    * What if they put me in a corner and ask a question? What am I to say?
  - The Third Insecurity—What if they don't believe me (see 4:1)?
    * The LORD gave him three signs: 1). A rod turning into a snake, 2). A leprous hand, and 3). The water becoming blood on dry land.
  - The Fourth Insecurity—*"I am not eloquent [a persuasive speaker]."* Instead, I am *"slow of speech and of a slow tongue"* (4:10).
    * The LORD answered, "I made your mouth. Go, and I will be with you." Moses still wanted to reject what the LORD was asking of him, causing the LORD's anger to rise against Moses. Moses wanted the LORD to send someone else (see 4:13).

What rises inside of me when I hear the LORD urging me to get active with my calling in the Kingdom?

_____
_____
_____

- Moses' wife, Zipporah, didn't go with him. There may be a time when the LORD needs to separate us from outside influences.
- Notice, in chapter 4, the LORD sought to kill Moses or, some believe, Moses' uncircumcised son. Did Moses circumcise one son to follow the LORD's commands, and NOT circumcise the other son, to please his wife? At a point in the story, Zipporah performed the circumci-

sion on her son herself and threw the foreskin at Moses' feet.
- Notice that for Moses to be a warrior and bring the Israelites to freedom, he first had to be obedient to the LORD God and face what had caused him to run!
- They went through the ten plagues, which are symbolic of the ten different gods that were dominant in that area and to that culture.
- The people were now free. They left Egypt and started what we call "the wilderness journey" (see chapters 13 and 14).
- In chapter 16, they started murmuring and complaining. The LORD then rained down manna for them to eat.

Read Exodus 17

17:1—Notice, the children of Israel were in the Wilderness of Sin.
Sin means "thorn." They were in the midst of a demonic battle.

17:4—Moses asked the LORD, *"What shall I do unto this people? they be almost ready to stone me?"*
Notice, when things went wrong, the people respond quickly by blaming Moses.

Do I take it personally when others reject the LORD through me?

_____
_____
_____

17:5-6—The LORD responded to Moses and told him to smite the rock to get water for the people.

17:7—Moses named that place Massah and Meribah, because of their chiding and because they tempted the LORD. They tempted the LORD by saying, *"Is the LORD among us, or not?"*
  Reference: 1 Corinthians 10:9

When I am in the middle of pressure or a battle, do I doubt the LORD's hand in it? How many times does the LORD have to prove Himself to me?

_____
_____
_____

17:11-13
- Notice that when Moses' hand was raised, the Israelites were winning the battle. When Moses' hand was lowered, Amalek started winning.
- Amalek was the grandson of Esau (see Genesis 36:12).
- The name Amalek means "dweller in a valley."
- The Amalekites were Esau's descendants.
- Esau sold his birthright for temporary pleasure. This was taking things lightly.
- Esau didn't believe his birthright would do him any good (see Genesis 25:32).

- Notice that Aaron and Hur saw Moses as weak, so they placed a stone under Moses, and he sat on it, while Aaron and Hur held his arms up.
    - *"Iron sharpens iron."*
    - *"Do not forsake the assembling of yourselves together."*

17:14—*"Write **this** for a memorial in a book."*
Why? This is our ability to pass down the LORD's commands, which is **His** remembrance!

17:15—Moses built an altar and named it Jehovah-Nissi.

17:16—The LORD swore that He would be at war with Amalek from generation to generation.

Matthew 16:26 asks us, *"What shall a man give in exchange for his soul?"*
- We can exchange a truth for a lie and serve the creature and not the Creator (see Romans 1:25).
- Satan is the one who trades within us (see Ezekiel 28:16).
- The LORD trades our mourning for dancing and our sackcloth for gladness (see Psalm 30:11).

What banner or standard in my life do I lower in exchange for temporary satisfaction?
- Do I lower my standard for a once-in-a-blue-moon date night or family get-together?
- Do I only pray when I am in need, only later to slack off when things are going well?
- Do I start reading and studying the Word, only to stop because I am tired or something came up that interests me more?
- If my attitude changes when the pastor is around, this could possibly show an area where I have lowered my standards.
- Do I lower the LORD's standard of unity because of a generational grudge?

_____
_____
_____

Do I talk positively about what I am praying for in front of other people, then, when I am alone, speak the opposite? I speak out of my heart. What is in my heart (that I believe about myself or the LORD God) that can cause me to bury my seed with words of doubt?

_____
_____
_____
_____
_____

Where have I had an opportunity or a test to see if I would continue in my forefather's grudge, bitterness, division, carrying the same type of behavior, or even the same way of making decisions?

_____
_____
_____
_____

Moses raised his hands to the LORD ... until he grew tired and needed the help of his friends. What standard or conviction do I get tired of holding up?

_____
_____
_____
_____

Think about a physical battle, when someone raises a white flag. White represents purity. A white flag waved in battle represents surrender. You surrender when you don't think you can make it and give up fighting. Moses' hands were raised to the LORD, giving Him glory and honor. Raising our hands is a sign of surrender. We surrender with our heart to the LORD. In those moments, we are focused on the LORD in the battle and not ourselves. When you lower your flag (your standard you live by), you are surrendering to something else other than the LORD. What you surrender to can become an idol that you heed above the LORD. This is spiritual idolatry.

What battle am I in that causes me to want to quit fighting and throw in the towel?

_____
_____
_____
_____

In what area or areas of my spiritual life have I lowered my flag by compromising my standards in order not to offend someone or stir up the water? Notice, did I struggle in that area afterward?

_____
_____
_____
_____

What standard or conviction do I lower over my home, opening my atmosphere to things that affect more than just me?

_____
_____
_____
_____

Are my speech and actions different around different groups of people?
Do I do something I would normally not do, lowering my standard and opening up my atmosphere?

_____
_____
_____
_____

Chapter 16

Our Atmosphere

Our atmosphere is affected by:
- What we allow in and out of our hedge
- What we see and discern
- What we tolerate by hearing something and then choosing to remain silent about it
- What we believe

We all pray for a hedge of protection.

If I were to ask you what a hedge of protection looked like, how would you define the word *hedge*?

_____
_____
_____

GOD'S HEDGE

Colossians 1:12-14
- God delivers us from the power of _____ and translates, or transfers, us into the Kingdom of His Son, Jesus!
- When we are saved and under a new covering, why then do we still have to struggle and continue to fight the attacks of Satan?
    ° We fight because of the two avenues **Satan** uses to attack us!

1. The Lord God gives _____ , then we can choose whether we accept the _____ .
    * Through an _____, you have the chance to accept the intrusion and to put yourself under a curse.
    * While going through the intrusion, we can start to heed the voices of our past idols, which is the iniquity. We can start to hear the fear of rejection (or whichever other idol we had) start screaming at us to stop and obey that voice over the Lord's. In Numbers 31:16, we see that through the counsel of Balaam, the people trespassed against the Lord, causing a plague to come upon them.

Maintaining Generational Freedom | 198

2. We or someone over us has given Satan _____ _____ in our lives.

A BROKEN HEDGE

Job 1:1—2:10

- In 1:6, Satan and the sons of God had to present themselves before the Lord.

- In 1:8-10, the Lord placed a _____ around Job and surrounded everything he owned.

- In 1:12, we see that the hedge was _____ _____ _____ _____.

If Satan cannot attack us without an opened door or permission, let's look harder at Job's story through this chapter.

- In 1:12, we see Satan getting _____ from the Lord.

- Notice that even if Satan had legal ground to stand on, he still needed permission. The Lord _____ how far Satan was able to attack Job.

But what was he getting permission for?

- In 1:13-19, we see that Satan was given permission for an _____ with hopes of an opportunity into Job's life.

Did the intrusion work?
Did Satan get the open door he was looking for?

- In 1:22, we see that Satan didn't receive _____ _____ into Job's life because the Scriptures say, *"Job sinned not, nor charged God foolishly."*
  ○ Job had been offered a chance to carry an offense and become bitter toward God, cursing Him to His face.

- In 2:3-5, we see Satan going to the Lord to get _____ again.

Notice, he didn't just send an intrusion again in the same area, hoping for a different result.

- In Job 2:6-7, we see that the Lord gave Satan _____ again. This permission was for a different type of _____ , to see if Job would give up his integrity and his moral principles, and stir up hatred against God.
  ○ How do you give your power and authority over to Satan?

- In 2:10, we see another failed attempt. Satan still didn't receive _____ _____ into Job's life. This scripture states, *"In all this did not Job sin with his lips."*
  ○ Notice, this time it doesn't say anything about him NOT charging God.

But what if we UNKNOWINGLY hold offenses, giving legal ground to Satan to ask God for permission to sift us? Grace covers us!

But what happens when we frustrate the grace of God and it lifts (see Galatians 2:21)?

What if we have a false perception of God, which is an iniquity?

Then the LORD brings us through a purging process for our own good, to cleanse our perception of Him.

What if we "mess up," and Satan has legal rights once again into our atmosphere?

Ecclesiastes 10:8

If I break my hedge or spiritual wall (my complete loyalty and trust in God that is around us), what happens?

_____
_____
_____

FIXING THE HEDGE

Ezekiel 13:3-5
- Here Ezekiel was warning the Israelite prophets, who falsely prophesied out of their own spirit, saying things through their own perception and interpretation of the Word!
- We call this being _____-_____.
- Ezekiel compared these people to jackals, which are _____ _____.
  ◦ What does the Bible say about small foxes?

_____

What happens if, by resisting the leading of the Holy Spirit, I fail to repair my hedge or the spiritual wall around me?

_____
_____
_____

Ezekiel 13:10-16
Vs. 10—You seduced My people and said there was peace when there wasn't.
  ◦ How do we seduce people by declaring peace when there isn't any true peace?
  ◦ Example: If I operate out of fear of rejection and _____, then I might seduce others and teach them to operate the same way I do.
  ◦ The Scriptures tell us to be peacemakers, not peacekeepers (see Matthew 5:9).
  ◦ We put up a wall or an image that everything is good when it truly is not.

Maintaining Generational Freedom | 200

Vs. 14—The wall falls so that the foundation is _____.
- ° What are the foundational lies our wall is built upon?

Luke 10:18-19 (words of Jesus)
Even if I re-open my hedge unknowingly, I have the _____ by faith in the power of the name of Jesus to close it because of the cross!
Jesus took back the _____ and _____ from Satan.

Authority overcomes the Power of Darkness EVERY TIME

There are three ways Satan is allowed to attack us!

John 10:10
*"The thief cometh not, but for to _____ and to _____, and to _____.
I am come that they might have life, and that they might have it more abundantly!"*

SATAN STEALS OUR PROPERTY THROUGH _____ _____.
- ° This operates in our life through vows, oaths, and soul-ties.
- ° This is our peace, time, money, or emotions, etc.
- ° Do we hand things over when we speak from the abundance of our heart, or do we stop and discern what others (perhaps unknowingly) speak over us or others?
- ° Satan steals our free will from us through manipulation, intimidation, and deception, when we allow offense to take root, handing over our free will and again returning to the same bondage we were delivered from (see Matthew 15:11).

SATAN KILLS OUR PHYSICAL HEALTH THROUGH _____ _____.
- ° This is through our habits, personality, or mindset.
- ° Our behavior and actions come through what we choose to believe about ourselves, others, and God.

SATAN DESTROYS OUR FAMILIES THROUGH _____ _____.
- ° This is ancestral and through our family lineage.
- ° These are learned behaviors, views of how to see or feel that we act upon and that are passed down to us.
- ° These are the iniquities of our forefathers that we are visited with. (Examples: racism, grudges, unforgiveness, etc.)

A HEDGE BY INHERITANCE OR MARRIAGE
(Our Personal Hedge)

MEN
Deuteronomy 21:15-17
- The first-born male was born with a _____ _____ of inheritance.
- This was both good and bad.
- We can make an exception, where the oldest does not receive the inheritance, because it is awarded by what we speak.

WOMEN
Numbers 27:8-11
- In a family where there was NO son, the inheritance went to the oldest daughter _____ marriage.

MARRIAGE
Mark 10:7-9
- Men carry the _____!
- Women get married and _____ _____ the husband's hedge.
  ◦ You can find a diagram, or picture, online where it shows the umbrella effect of the correct order of submission.
    * Christ, then the husband, next the wife, then the children (see Ephesians 5:22-24).
- For the women, think about your struggles, feelings or emotions before marriage compared to after marriage. Did they change?

Ruth 1
Why did Naomi leave Bethlehem with worth but return with none?

_____
_____
_____

How do you think Naomi felt? She had started out with a good life, married, with children, and a comfortable existence. Then, all of a sudden, she found herself in poverty, broken and probably not feeling like she had much worth or value.

In 1:19-21, Naomi, which means "my delight, pleasant," found herself blaming the Lord. She then changed her name to Mara, which means "bitter."
- Naomi didn't stop believing in the Lord but possibly carried an offense in how she saw Him.

Have I possibly found myself in a place like Naomi, where I have tasted bitterness? How did it change me and how I see things?

___

___

___

___

___

In Ruth 4:15, we see that Ruth was restored.

THE HEDGE OF OUR SURROUNDINGS

Leviticus 18:24-28
Why was the land defiled and the Lord God said, *"THEREFORE I DO VISIT THE INIQUITY THEREOF UPON IT?"*

___

___

___

Jeremiah 3:1-9
Why was the land greatly polluted and defiled?

___

___

___

Isaiah 24:4-6
Why was the land defiled and cursed?

___

___

___

HOW DID JOB CLOSE THE BREACH IN HIS HEDGE?

#1 – THE _____ _____, WHICH OPERATES THROUGH _____ _____ WHAT IS HAPPENING

The steal door is opened by being _____-_____. We are soul-led when we take matters into our own hands. Adam stole wisdom instead of asking the LORD God for it.

Job 1:5
- Job made sacrifices on his children's behalf.
- He said, *"It may be that my sons have sinned, and cursed God in their hearts. Thus did Job continually."*
- Job had a fear that his children were sinning in their hearts. He was responding on their behalf, offering a sacrifice for them.

What fears do I have that can control me strongly, causing me to respond to what reality shows me instead of trusting that God can use that trial or circumstance to help us grow?

_____

_____

_____

Job had to be willing to look _____ himself.
- Thinking about the culture Job lived in at the time, did that generation have a wrong view of the LORD God?
  - The LORD said to Satan, *"Still he holdeth fast his integrity, although thou movedst me against him, to destroy him without a cause"* (Job 2:3).
  - Satan used Job's wife for an opportunity for intrusion (Job 2:9).
  - By using Numbers 30:6-8, Job dealt with this matter in the physical and in the spiritual.
  - Job saw God as the One who blesses and punishes those who serve Him (Job 2:10).

- The LORD confronted him for dealing treacherously with his friends.
  - Eliphaz (possibly the son of Esau) had a vision from God in Job 4:13-21. Job couldn't receive from his friends.
  - Job 9 shows us how Job became offended with his friends' counsel. Offense will limit God talking to us through others.

Maintaining Generational Freedom | 204

- Job 40:8—The Lord confronted Job for dealing treacherously with Him.
  ◦ 6:4—Job saw his tragedy as the Lord God attacking him, saw the arrows as being from the Lord. *"For the arrows of the Almighty are within me, the poison whereof drinketh up my spirit: the terrors of God do set themselves in array against me."*
    * This scripture shows how they all viewed the Lord God, which could have caused Job to first make sacrifices on behalf of his children (Job 4:9 and 8:4).
    * This was the belief of the god Baal. In their time and their generational culture, Baal required child sacrifice to atone for their sins.
  ◦ 7:11-21—Did Job possibly see God as the One who was targeting him?
  ◦ 8:1-7—Job's friend, Bildad, discussed God's character through his own understanding of Him and brought up Job's children.

- The first attack Job went through was outward.

- The second attack Job went through was inward.

#2 – THE _____ WHICH OPERATES THROUGH THE _____.

WE NEED TO TRADE THE LIE (the offense or perception we believe, whether about ourselves, others, or even the Lord God) BACK TO THE LORD GOD'S TRUTH, SO THAT WE CAN RETURN OUR WORSHIP TO THE CREATOR (see Romans 1:25).

- Job 42:1-6—The Lord brought Job from head knowledge to _____ knowledge.
  ◦ *"I have heard of thee [referring to God] by the hearing of the ear: but now my eye seeth thee. Wherefore I abhor myself and repent in dust and ashes."*
    * Job applied heart circumcision!

What does it mean by saying that Job knew the Lord God by the hearing of the ear, but now his eyes had seen God?

_____
_____
_____

- Job 42:7-8—Who the Lord would now accept.
  ◦ Job dealt with the offenses he had harbored against the Lord God Himself. The Lord was now asking him to deal with the offenses he may have held against his friends.

- What did Job do, resulting in his prayer being heard, received, and answered?
  ◦ Job opened himself up and allowed heart circumcision to take place both _____ and _____.

Our Atmosphere | 205

#3 – THE _____ _____ OPERATES IN THE _____. THIS IS THE _____ WE TAKE.

Why did Job have to pray for his friends (reference: Psalm 133:1-3 and Acts 24:16)?

_____

_____

- Matthew 10:1-8—When the twelve disciples became apostles
  - They were sent out in pairs (we are not meant to do things on our own).
  - Jesus told them not to go to the Gentiles, but to the lost sheep of the House of Israel, the Jews.

- Luke 4:18-19—Three things they were told to do **WITH THE LOST SHEEP**:
  - Preach the Gospel
    (RELEASES PEOPLE FROM BEING A _____)
  - Heal the sick, cleanse the lepers, raise the dead.
    (SET OTHERS FREE FROM _____)
  - Cast out devils
    (HEART CIRCUMCISION WHICH BRINGS YOU TO _____)

- John 20:19-31
  - *"Peace be to unto you!"* Jesus breathed on them and said in verse 22-23:
    "Receive ye the Holy Ghost: whose soever sins ye remit, they are remitted unto them; and whose soever sins ye retain, they are retained."
  - The word *retain* refers to "taking hold of something and keeping it."
  - In verse 29, it states, *"Blessed are they that have not seen, and yet have believed."*
  - In verse 31, it states, *"And that believing ye might have life through HIS NAME."*

- Once Job shut all three doors, things instantly manifested!

Job 42:10

*"THE LORD **TURNED** THE CAPTIVITY OF JOB,*
__WHEN__ HE PRAYED FOR HIS FRIENDS."

Peace returned to Job, and he was no longer retaining offense or unforgiveness.
Notice that his captivity was turned.
He was no longer a prisoner.
He had been held captive because of what he believed.
In the beginning, he believed that God was attacking him.
Now he had a new, clearer perception of the Lord his God and knew that the Lord was his Restorer!

AFTERWORD

What we have presented in these pages are some tools that, if used properly and regularly, can help you maintain your freedom. Our hope is that you continue journaling daily from God's living Word and allow the Holy Spirit to transform your mind, enabling you to develop a lifestyle and habit of seeking Him diligently. This study has not only brought us to a lifestyle change but was designed to bring others to the same lifestyle change! Let it happen through you.

Crystal Callais and Lorraine Foret

If you would like to anonymously email your list of breakthroughs and revelations to <u>maintainingfreedom@yahoo.com</u>, we would love to hear what the Lord your God has done for you through the guidance of the Holy Spirit in this study, and we can add you to the list!

Other Books by Crystal Callais and Lorraine Foret

Do you find yourself struggling with unanswered prayers and unanswered questions? With family unity? With fulfilling your call in God? With maintaining your peace, assurance, self-worth, or self-respect? Are you looking for a deeper, more intimate walk with Jesus Christ, your Lord and Savior? Join us as we journey from Genesis through Revelation, allowing the Holy Spirit to reveal to us a deeper understanding of who the Lord truly is; He is LOVE!

We will discuss patterns, mindsets and broken covenants that stand in our way, preventing us from fully experiencing what is ours. Our hope is that you will see how these mindsets, which are strongholds, pass from one generation to the next and how to stop them in their tracks and not allow them to continue down your family line.

Total freedom is possible for you! Through this course, you will learn how to maintain the freedom that was purchased at such a high price with the BLOOD of Jesus Christ on the cross of Calvary.

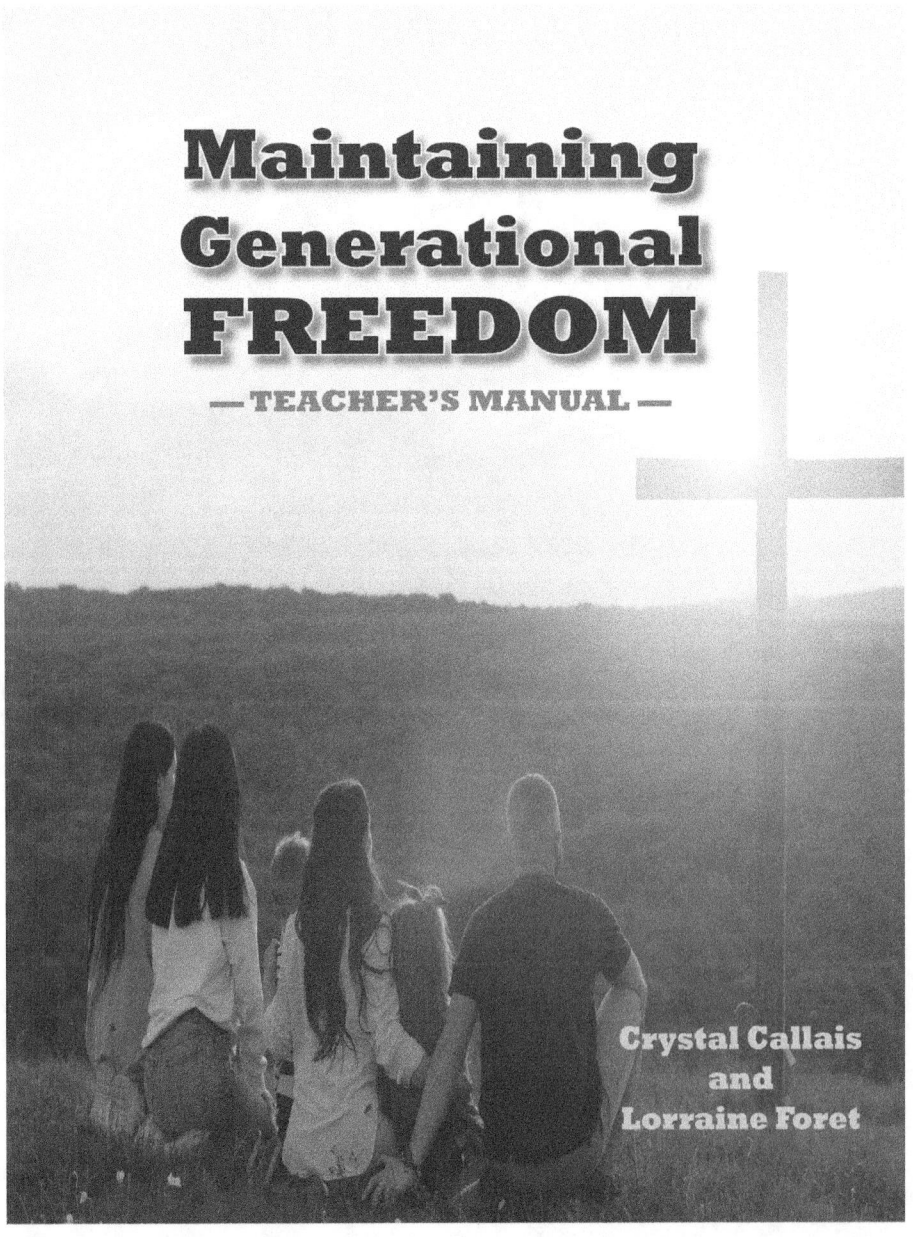

There are times in our lives when we become stagnant and have a hard time breaking the repetitiveness that we have fallen into. This devotional was inspired to aid in bringing a fresh and deeper thought process into the study of God's Word. His will is that we continually have a fresh revelation of Him and see everything from His perspective, not our own. Crystal has included questions that will challenge you to think outside of your normal thought process or "out of the box." Allow every part of this devotional to be thought provoking, while positioning yourself to be vulnerable before God. If you do that, He will bring you into new depths in your relationship with Him, and you will find yourself ***Going Deeper.***

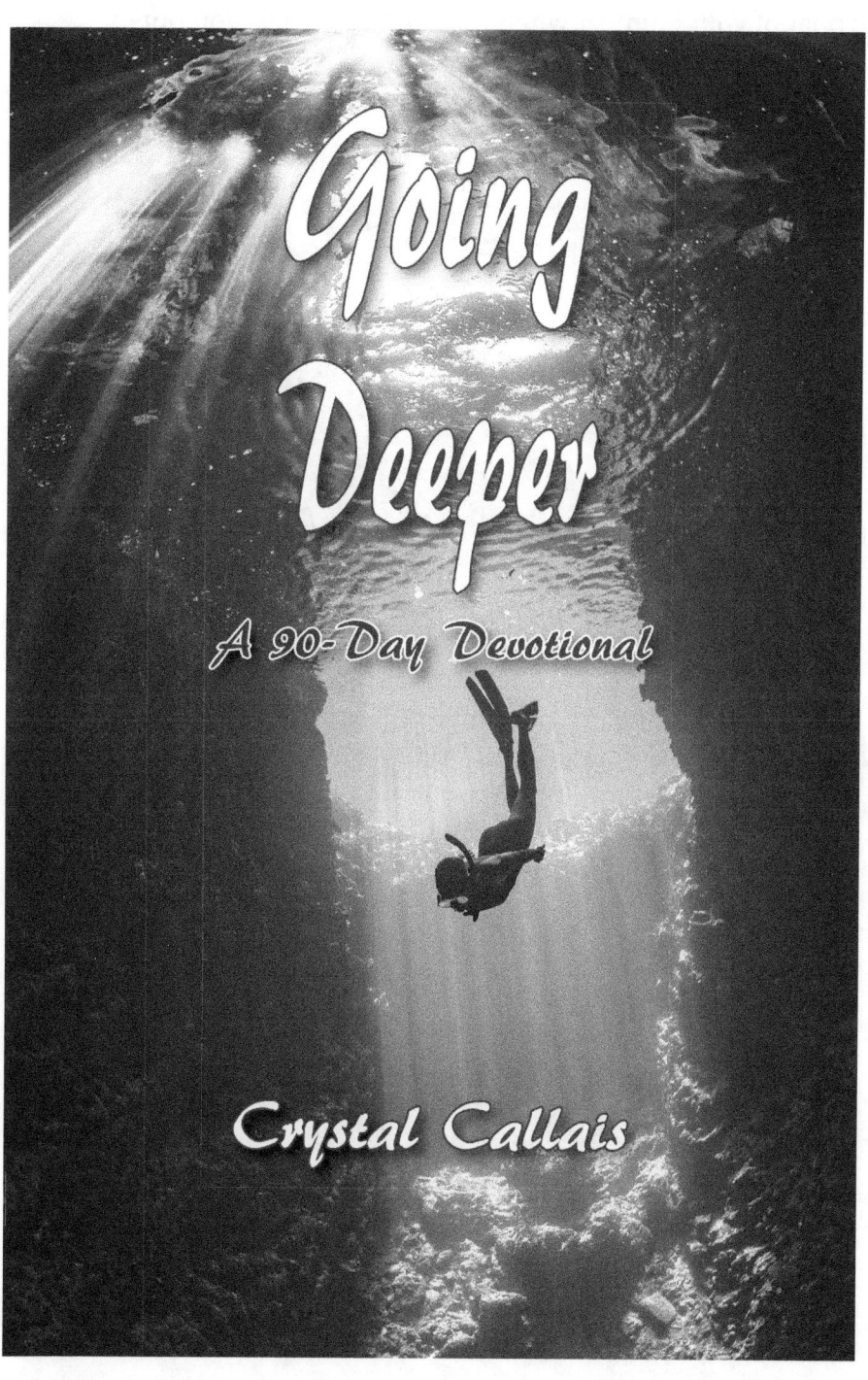

We all have a boat of comfort we tend to navigate life through, and there are moments in life when the Lord God calls us to step out of our comfort zone and do things we are not always comfortable with. At times, the water is calm and peaceful, so stepping out of the boat in obedience to what He has asked of us is easy. But what if there is a storm present? What if the water seems rough, making it harder to step out of our comfort zone when the Lord asks us to? In these times, we need to grow and stretch our faith in the Lord God so that we can step out in obedience. Take this journey and grow your faith. This study can be used with some friends as a small group study or as a personal growth plan. Crystal will lead you through scripture references and stories to help build your faith, enabling you to step out the boat of your comfort when the Lord God calls you out.

AUTHOR CONTACT PAGE

You may contact Crystal Callais or Lorraine Foret by email at:

maintainingfreedom@yahoo.com

www.ingramcontent.com/pod-product-compliance
Lightning Source LLC
Chambersburg PA
CBHW080732230426
43665CB00020B/2709